TALES THAT IGNITE
THE IMAGINATION

WHY GEESE FLY FARTHER THAN EAGLES

Bob Stromberg

Publishing
Colorado Springs, Colorado

WHY GEESE FLY FARTHER THAN EAGLES
Copyright © 1992 Bob Stromberg

Library of Congress Cataloging-in-Publication Data
Stromberg, Bob, 1952–
    Why geese fly farther than eagles / Bob Stromberg.
       p.   cm.
    ISBN 1-56179-074-5
    1. Outdoor life—Fiction. I. Title.
    PS3569.T6973W48   1992   92-1323
    813'.54—dc20   CIP

Published by Focus on the Family Publishing, Colorado Springs, CO 80995

Distributed in the U.S.A. and Canada by Word Books, Dallas, Texas.

Editor: Janet Kobobel
Cover design: Steve Diggs and Friends

Printed in the United States of America

92 93 94 95 96 97 / 10 9 8 7 6 5 4 3 2 1

To my grandfather Albin Nelson,
who to the very end loved to tell me stories.
I wish now I'd listened more intently.

CONTENTS

ACKNOWLEDGMENTS

Many names have been changed, of course, sometimes to protect the innocent, sometimes to protect the guilty, and once or twice to protect me. Other times I've used actual names just because I thought the people I wrote about would enjoy it.

I wish to acknowledge all the real folk who live in these pages. Regardless of what I've called you, I hope you recognize yourselves and delight in these stories, which are yours, too.

I'd like to thank my good friend Chuck Bolte at Focus on the Family who said, "Let me introduce you to Janet Kobobel."

I'd like to thank my editor, Janet Kobobel, for her honest criticism, sweet spirit and continual encouragement as I worked on this book. I especially appreciate that she was wrong once or twice, which made me very pleased—in fact, nearly euphoric.

I'd like to thank my parents, Bob and Lucielle Stromberg, who always believed my profession as a storyteller to be a noble one. They can only imagine how much this has meant to me through the years.

I'd like to thank my wife, Judy, and my boys, Nate and Lars. Judy read many rough drafts and helped me to answer some difficult questions like "What is a complete sentence, anyway?" All three of them sacrificed a lot of evening and weekend hours with me so this book could happen. They are truly a delight and joy for which I am daily grateful.

And I'd like to thank you, the reader, for picking up this book. I hope you will have a "wonder filled" time as you read these tales.

CHAPTER ONE

BOULDERS IN THE TOPSOIL

My paternal grandfather grew up in the province of Småland in southern Sweden. It is to this day a beautiful land of misty white birch, fields of buttercups and stone walls everywhere. The walls are not decorative like those in New England. The walls in Småland are big, five feet tall and six feet across the top, stretching field after field, and longer every year.

Each spring the fields yield an abundance of new boulders. The farmers harvest this crop they did not sow and pile it higher along the walls to plant crops in preparation for a more fruitful harvest. This hard land was my grandfather's home.

Barely more than a boy, my grandfather embraced his mom and dad for the last time and left those rocky fields of tiny potatoes, dreaming of deeper, darker, American soil. The fields he dreamed of were probably in Minnesota, but he had no idea how vast his new country was.

1

By the time he reached western Pennsylvania, years had past. He now knew the love of a young woman, his wife, who spoke his language. He knew the joy and worrisome responsibility of young children. He knew the hopeless monotony of American factories and the sweat of the oil fields. And he knew the ache in an immigrant's heart. An ache for which there was no remedy.

One day he saw a sight that filled him with a joy he'd almost forgotten. A "For Sale" sign stood in the yard of a farm nestled on a hillside. The house didn't look like much. It was far too small for his growing family, but it was every bit as good as what he'd known in Sweden, maybe better. There was plenty of good lumber to build a barn. The few fields that had been cleared were dark soil, and most wonderfully, everywhere there were boulders. As far as he could see there were boulders, thousands of boulders. It was the most beautiful sight he'd seen in years. He was finally home in America.

My father grew up on that farm, sharing the tiny house with his mom and dad, three sisters, two brothers and a grandma. Though it was a tough life, I think my grandparents must have communicated to my dad the joy of this place that was their own, a little farmhouse, nestled on the hillside, surrounded by rocks.

My father in turn instilled in me an excitement about the place. Though we frequently piled in the Studebaker and drove through the countryside to the farm, it was always a special occasion to me, almost a sacred connection to something deep within.

It probably had something to do with my first sense of belonging to a community. We hardly ever went to the farm and found ourselves the only guests. All my father's family would be there. All my cousins, most of whom were older than I, would be waiting when we arrived. I was privileged in a way. Lots of babies and toddlers were around, but I was just old enough to be the youngest of the big kids.

My grandmother could make a feast out of almost nothing and feed the whole bunch. It was her specialty. After the meal, as our parents drank coffee and the evening shadows crossed the valley and covered the farmhouse, the children piled out the door to chase fireflies or play Kick the Can.

The older kids went in the barn after dark, daring me to do the same. But I preferred to stay close to the back light, close to the reassuring laughter and conversation just inside the kitchen door.

I especially remember a late autumn evening when I learned something about the sanctity of life. As the kids flew out the screen door to play, it was already pitch dark, and fireflies seemed a distant memory. Once again, by some mysterious process of adding up fingers on our hands, I found myself face to the wall, counting to one hundred as cousins scattered like quail across the yard, behind trees and around the farmhouse.

"Ninety-eight, ninety-nine, one hundred. Here I come, ready or not!" I spun around, took one step and froze, my eyes and mouth wide open.

There before me, not five feet away, just inside the circle of light, with an expression on his face much like my own, was the largest rat I'd ever seen. In fact, it was the only rat I'd ever seen. The light through the kitchen curtains made him strangely yellow.

We stared at each other long enough for me to feel embarrassed, as if maybe I should start a conversation. Then the rat smiled. It really did. It started to back away and then smiled as if to say, "Whoops. I didn't expect to run into you like this. Just remain calm, and I'll sort of slip away."

Out of the darkness, with the cry of warriors, cousins shot past me for the goal. They tripped over the startled rat, which tumbled into the center of the light, now surrounded by screaming children.

The oldest boy sprang to his feet and flung his lanky body against the house. "Look at the size of that thing! Somebody get a stick."

The rat, realizing that timing was everything, shot between two boys who, interpreting this as an offensive move, let out a junior high squawk and kicked at their attacker. Stunned, the rat tried to run across the stony drive, but like a prancing kitten, its hind legs seemed to go off on their own.

"Somebody get a stick! Quick! It's going to get away!"

"Hey, you kids, no fighting out there, and no playing with sticks. Do you hear me?"

The rat was nearly to the edge of the driveway. Another couple of feet and it would be in the field and gone. I'd never known such fear and exhilaration, my heart pounding, "A rat, a rat, a rat, a rat!"

"Where is the *stick*?!" someone shouted.

As if from another world, I heard my father's voice. "What's going on out there?"

One of the boys, half a yard away, shot through the barn door with a shovel. I had not moved a step this whole time, my eyes tracking the big yellow pelt, the rushing in my ears pulsing out, "A rat, a rat, a rat!"

Cousins were hopping about screaming, "Don't let him get away! Quick! Kick him back in!"

"Bobby, what's going on out there?"

"A rat, a rat!" I don't remember picking up the stone. I was a full twenty feet away, but there was never a doubt in my mind.

The stone flew from my hand, whizzed close past my cousins, fell two feet short of its target, skipped over the dirt and hit the rat right in the face. The rat lay dead.

All my older cousins looked at me in disbelief. "What a shot! Right in the head! Can you believe it?! Way to go!"

The screen door was opening. My father was saying something.

"Dad, I killed a rat. Should have seen it. Hit him right in the head."

And then everything changed. My body, drained from the pumping adrenaline, went weak. My cousins became oddly quiet and started to fade off into the shadows. Those close to the house quickly let themselves in the back door.

"Bobby, what have you done? Oh, what have you done?"

"I killed a rat, Dad. I just picked up the stone and hit it right in the head, from way over here."

The words were no more out of my mouth than I wished I could bring them back. Something was terribly wrong. My father stood over the rat, his face contorting.. For the first time in my life I saw tears in his eyes.

"How could you do this, son? It's a baby possum."

The words were like a blow to my chest, and then the sobs rose from deep inside.

"Oh, Dad, I didn't mean it. I mean, I didn't know it was . . . Oh, Dad, I'm sorry. I'm so sorry."

My dad picked up the shovel, lifted the little creature off the stones and carried it into the dark field.

He didn't punish me. He knew it wasn't necessary. And though I never doubted he had forgiven me, this memory still comes back from time to time. When I feel the rushing adrenaline of jealousy or anger or bitterness or revenge rise in my soul, this memory surfaces to my consciousness like a boulder pushing through the topsoil.

"Oh, Father, forgive me," I pray.

And then, once again, He helps me lift the rock onto the wall, and we go on preparing for the harvest.

CHAPTER TWO

ON GLOSSY
BOOKS AND
FORGIVENESS

My wife and I appreciate that my mother is not a stereotypical grandma. She's looking the part more each year, with her beautiful white hair and soft skin on the back of her arms. And she acts the part well, pinching our children's cheeks and saying things like "You're just growing up right before my eyes" and "Where's that hug for your grandma?" But we're thankful that her behavior at least in one respect strays from the grandma-norm. My mother doesn't buy our children candy; she buys them books.

She always has, even before our children were born. Sometimes they would arrive by truck in big, heavy boxes, more books than the kids would read should they seek Ph.D.'s. When the children were very young, the books were mostly vinyl, with few words. Then came soft-covered, still relatively inexpensive books. Then a few hardback, more expensive books, and I wondered if my mom could continue what she had begun.

7

Eventually she stopped sending product and instead sent brochures and order blanks that could be filled out and sent directly to the companies. This way she could be billed directly and have the satisfaction of knowing her grandchildren were getting books they wanted to read.

This, of course, was guilt inducing for my wife and me, as our children, attracted to the most colorful ads, chose more and more expensive books.

One November day our fourth grader came home from school, threw his book bag up on the counter and began to open a letter from his grandma. As he gulped down a glass of chocolate milk, he said, "Look it here, you guys, another book order. I wonder if there's anything here we don't already have."

It only took a glance for him to realize this brochure was something different. "Whoa, look at this."

No kiddie books here. Only large, hardback, glossy-paper beauties. The ad had pictures of a book on astronomy with color photos of the Horse Head Nebula. There was a four-hundred-pager on Egyptian mummies. There was one on the history of air travel from Leonardo da Vinci to the present day. I knew my mom had either won the lottery or lost her mind. There was not a book to be ordered for under twenty-eight dollars.

My son's jaw dropped, and his eyes glazed over. "Oh, Dad," he said, gazing at the brochure. "Oh, Dad, look at this."

It wasn't necessary for me to look. I knew this child. I knew he had decided to order the most expensive one. It was the kind of oversized book people put on expensive coffee tables. It was an inch and a half thick, probably weighing ten pounds. It was the kind of book I used to have to work nights to pay for when I was in college. It was a book on killer sharks.

I phoned my mom, who sounded quite normal. She said it would be fine for my son to order that book, though perhaps it would be best if, just this time, he selected only one.

The company guaranteed the book would be delivered in six weeks. It wasn't. In fact, it had not arrived in six months.

When I was a child, I'm certain I would have forgotten about that book after a couple of weeks. When I finally did receive it, I would be overjoyed, and the surprise would be better than if I had anticipated getting the book for all those months. I knew that would not be the way with my son.

"Did it come yet?" he would say, bursting through the door everyday after school.

"Sorry, not today."

"Well, where is it? Do you think they forgot all about it? Could you call the post office? Maybe they lost it. Maybe they sent it to Grandma's. Maybe she didn't pay on time."

This went on until mid-April, when the truck finally pulled up in the driveway with the prize. By our son's reaction, you would have thought he had been told by his teacher that, because of his exceptional grades and exemplary attitude, he did not need to go to school any longer. Unless, of course, he'd like to stop over now and then, play a little kick ball, or help out at recess.

I was surprised to see that he didn't tear open the box. He opened it the way his mother would open a gift she knew to be fine crystal.

I must admit the book was beautiful. All evening we sat together on the sofa. I had to hold myself from flipping through the pages until my son had absorbed every photo.

Right before bed he said, "Dad, I think I better call Grandma. Don't you?"

She had no idea how happy she had made this little boy.

The next morning, I had to go to Minnesota. I had been away a lot over the last several weeks and wasn't looking forward to the trip.

But I was grateful my flight didn't leave until ten, which would allow me to have breakfast with my family and see the children off to school.

When we awakened that morning, it was a typically messy April morning in western Massachusetts. A wet snow was falling on the first spring leaves. Each flake was about three inches and was the kind that would make a sound if you let it hit you on the head.

My son came down the stairs half an hour early, wide awake and ready to go. Under his arm was the new book.

"I'm taking it to school, Dad. I can't believe it. I've been waiting for this morning all year. Mrs. Plummley is really going to love it."

"That's great, son," I said. "Just make sure you cover it up so it doesn't get all wet."

"I'm going to see if we can have a special Show and Tell just for me, so I can share it with the class."

"Sounds good, son," I said. "Why don't we try to put that inside your backpack?"

"Never fit, Dad. I'll just keep it under my arm."

He was flipping through the pages now. "Also, it's no big deal if I can't do Show and Tell, 'cause I can always show it to my buddies during recess."

Apparently I was not communicating effectively. In my most caring tone I tried again: "You know, there's no way you can take that outside during recess. Have you looked outside today?"

"No big deal, Dad."

"Oh, but it is, son." My tone became a little more urgent. "Have you seen those snowflakes? They're the kind that knock you over when they hit you. They each weigh about a pound, and they're full of water . . ."

"It'll be okay, Dad, really."

"No, no, it won't be okay. One of those snowflakes will ruin a page. That's an expensive book. How would your grandma—"

My son interrupted in a tone too much like my own. "Dad, I can't do anything about the weather. Okay!?"

"Ah ha, yes, that's right," I countered, "but you can do something about the book. Here's an idea. Let's put the book in a Baggie."

He looked at me as if I'd just asked him to wear platform shoes. "Dad, you've got to be kidding. No way! I'm not taking my book in a *Baggie.*"

I was losing it now. "Then you're not taking the book."

"Then I'm not going to school."

"Then you're not keeping the book."

His expression was one of dumbfounded disbelief. He just stood there. What a comeback I'd made, and I never even raised my voice! My wife had to be proud of me. I had him fair and square. What could he say?

He said what was on his mind. "Dad, sometimes you are so *stupid!*"

That was it. I took the book and informed him we would discuss this problem when I returned from my trip to Minnesota, and in the meantime, he had better be off to school.

I watched him stomp down the drive, fists at his side, hat off his head, a deliberate act of defiance. His head was already soaked. Everything in his bearing screamed, "I hate my dad!"

It takes most of the day to fly to Minnesota from New England. It was important for me to work the whole way on my presentation. My paperwork said I would be speaking to about a thousand parents. My topic was "Discipline: The Key to a Harmonious Home."

When I got off the plane, I went directly to a phone.

"Oh, hi." It was my wife's voice. "I thought you might call. There's a young man here who's been waiting by the phone."

I heard a small voice, choking back tears. "Hello, Dad? I want to tell you I'm so sorry about the way I acted . . . and about what I said, and . . . I'm just so sorry."

"I understand, son. We'll sit down and talk about it just as soon as I get back, okay?"

"Oh, and Dad," the voice was starting to break apart now. "You know at recess? I didn't even play with the other kids."

I could hear the tears beginning. "You know that spot by the parking lot where you can look out past the corner of the post office and see the edge of our driveway? I just stood right there. And I did the same at noon recess and in the afternoon, too. Mrs. Plummley asked me if I was okay, and I told her I just wanted to be by myself for a while."

"Son, why did you do that?"

Through hard sobs came his answer. "Dad, I just kept looking at the driveway, because I was sure you would come."

My heart ached. "But you knew I couldn't come. You knew I had to go away."

I could hardly hear his voice now. "I know, Dad, but I just needed so much for you to come. I'm so sorry, Dad. Please, can you forgive me?"

From a thousand miles away, with tears in my eyes I said, "Yes, son. I love you. I forgive you."

The heart of this father was broken. My son, for the first time, felt the pain of spiritual separation from his dad. A separation that he had brought on himself. A separation only his father could restore. And for one long, wet day in April his father was not there.

As I walked through the airport, the tears on my face were not only for my son but also for me. How often I have felt the despair of separation from my heavenly Father, separation imposed by my own behavior. How often I have stood just outside the celebration of life, carrying a burden of guilt, wondering if God could possibly forgive me. How often I have ached like my son, longing for the embrace of his dad.

I wondered, *Could it be that God longs to hold me in His arms even as I long to embrace my boy*?

What is sweeter than reconciliation? What is more liberating than forgiveness? What is more awesome than a God who need not call long distance?

CHAPTER THREE

WHY GEESE FLY FARTHER THAN EAGLES

I 'd never seen a bird so large, so near.
But, clearly ill, she landed here,
Indeed, nearly dead.
I fed her some and then said,
"You may stay here, if you choose."
And that's how she became "my" goose.

At least I said she was mine.
I suppose she was for a short time,
until she was stronger, when I set her free.
But for a while she stayed with me.

No eagle claw, hooked beak or furrowed brow.
Of these things she had no need,

13

for she was content
to fill herself on things among the weed,
and down around the small fish.
That's a dainty dish—
if you're a goose.

That is not to say, however,
and it would be wrong to think of her as weak,
not strong like the eagle.
For though the eagle is stronger in the fight,
more fit for the kill,
my goose can fly farther and longer
than any eagle will.

Oh, I've heard much lofty talk
about the eagle, falcon and hawk.
And it's not my desire,
nor would I conspire, to pull those big birds down.
Who would dare?
For when I watch them flying so high up there,
sometimes but a solitary dot,
I can but gaze in wonder and utter,
"My, look at that!"

But, as I've implied,
whether in the trees or in the sky,
eagles, falcons and hawks are almost always alone,
or at most in twos.
And that's what separates those birds
from my goose.

I suppose those in Iowa or Nebraska
would know it best,
for the sky is bigger
as you head toward the west.
But even as a lad nestled in the Alleghenies,
I looked forward, each fall, to seeing as many
as a thousand geese arrowing into view
over autumn ember elm and maple
and white birch, too.

One day, lying alone in the lawn on my back,
hearing only the sound of a distant train
on some far-off track,
I saw before my eyes,
ten thousand feet high or more,
a sight which to this day, I must say,
I've seen nothing like before.

The head goose,
the leader of the V,
suddenly veered out,
leaving a vacancy,
which was promptly filled by a bird behind.
The former leader then flew alongside
(the formation continued to grow wide),
and he found himself a spot at the back of the line.
They never missed a beat!

Well,
I was on my feet,
gaping mouth,

gazing south,
wondering what on earth I'd seen.
I told my friends.
They said, "So?"
I said, " 'So!'
What do you mean, 'So'?
Have you ever seen anything like that before?
      Mark?
           Jay?
                Paul?"
They said, "No, but don't be a bore;
let's go to the park and play ball."
So we did.
And that was that.

Well, now I'm an adult,
and I'm very busy.
I suppose that's a part of being grown.
But the point is, I hardly ever have time alone.
Not least,
lying in the lawn looking for geese.
And if I do see some, it's more or less luck.
Or I'll see a goose, but it's really a duck.
I might glimpse one up high while I'm stuck in traffic.
And that's why I'm thankful for the *National Geographic*.
For it tells me what I now tell you.
And if you don't believe what I say is true,
Then you can go look it up.

What I witnessed that day as a child
has been going on with geese in the wild

since the very first autumn.
You see, their bodies are streamlined,
the neck like a spear,
slicing the wind,
breaking the air.
And from the ground it's impossible to see,
but their wings aren't flapping randomly.

When the head goose grabs the wind,
air is displaced,
which then rushes up to reclaim its space,
only to see the smiling face
of the bird flying behind,
whose wings just happen to be in the downward position—
a very dangerous condition,
which doesn't last for long,
Because the upward rush
gives them a push,
and they're right back up where they belong.
This goose then grabs the air again,
causing another upward wind,
which lifts the bird behind.
And so and so it goes on down the line.

So the head goose breaks the wind,
and all the rest are carried by him,
with very little effort, I've heard,
on the part of any one bird.
When the head goose has had enough,
he or she simply drops back
and depends on another bird for strength
when strength is what is lacked.

So that's how I found out
how the goose can fly from up north
to way down south and back again.
But she cannot do it alone, you see.
It's something that must be done in community.

These days it's a popular notion,
and people swell with emotion and pride
when they think of themselves on the eagle-side.
      Solitary,
             Self-sufficient,
                    Strong.

But we are what we are.
That's something we cannot choose.
Though many would wish to be seen as an eagle,
I think God made most like the goose.

CHAPTER FOUR

A FATHER'S LOVE

M y father held the front car door and gingerly eased me into the seat. With numb confusion I stared at the misshapened arm cradled against my chest.

It looked remarkably unlike my own. On my wrist a large, soft dent forced my discoloring fingers into a useless, atrophied shape.

In my eight long years, I'd never experienced anything like this. I felt no pain but somehow knew that to be a temporary condition. Too much information had undoubtedly shot through my nerves at the same time. All the circuits were temporarily busy, but this call would be taken by the next available agent. Then my arm would be given my brain's complete and undivided attention.

Everything had happened so quickly. One moment I had been swinging through the high branches, and the next I was lying on my back, staring up at shimmering leaves. And the leaves were singing, or the closet was full of colored construction paper, crayons and even a bottle of glitter (the first I'd ever seen).

"Mom, come quick!" the choir sang.

"He's dead! He's dead!" they cried, followed by the squeaks and slams of a thousand screen doors and the converging faces of my hovering family.

Then I was sitting in the car, gazing on my arm as I might a broken pet.

My father looked ill.

"How's it feel, son?" he asked, slowing for even the smallest bumps. "Is it hurting you yet?"

"No, Dad, I think it's going to . . ."

Then the operator in my brain seemed to say, through a fiber-optically-clear connection, "I'm sorry to keep you waiting. I'll put your call through now."

Only moments before I had actually wondered if this bent thing belonged to me. Now, with each heartbeat, my arm throbbed away any doubt.

Reeling, I sobbed, "Oh, please, Dad, can't you do something? Oh, it hurts so bad! I don't think I can stand it!"

The words my father spoke shocked me only a little less than the fall. "Son," he said, his eyes reflecting every bit of my hurt, "I wish I could take the pain of that broken arm right out of your body and into my own."

My mind strained to take in this thought. Could this possibly be? Could he possibly know what he was saying? Did he have any idea how badly I ached?

"If I could, Bobby, I'd take every bit of it for you."

At that moment, with my body partly broken, my spirit was never more assured of my father's love. Though I couldn't understand, I believed him.

Several times during later years, long after this arm and other bones had healed, I openly questioned my dad's sincerity. "Ah, come on, Dad, be serious. You probably would have taken it for a few minutes, maybe given me a little rest. But you would have given it back."

My dad never backed down. "Someday, Bob, you'll understand."

And what do you know, he was right. Twenty-five years later on a bright, late-winter afternoon, his words came true.

My young family and I had been suffering for about a week. In fact, it seemed as though our whole little New England town had the fever. Peter Litchfield, the postmaster, said he couldn't remember a worse bout in recent times. He said he almost skipped work, which would have been the first time in nearly twenty-five years. His wife told him she'd move before she'd go through it again.

People in warmer climes will have difficulty understanding the severity of spring fever. One moment you're wet with sweat, longing to get outside, and the next you're shaking with chills of depression, knowing you'll probably have to wait another month.

To make things worse, the personality of this particular winter had created an even more oppressive strain of virus. We'd had snow the way I remember it as a child. Drifts had swept up, covering the lower panes of the first-story windows. Ice a half-inch thick had covered all the trees, transforming our town into a sparkling fairyland.

Unfortunately, the snow continued to fall until the trees had had enough. All the maples lost their top branches; many old oaks split down the middle and crashed to the ground.

Now, on a bright March day, with the melted snow revealing all the casualties, our town looked broken. I had the afternoon off, and recognizing that hard, outdoor labor is about the best remedy for spring fever, I decided the time had come to clean up the yard.

My four-year-old was thrilled to help. Several weeks earlier he had been to the market with his mother and bought a plastic kite at the checkout counter. Unfortunately he'd been unable to use it, as our lawn was, for him, an impenetrable jungle of branches.

So we bundled up, me in my old jeans and hooded sweatshirt, my boy in his boots, snow pants, sweatshirt, knit sweater-jacket, mittens, scarf and ear-flapped hat, which tied tightly under his chin.

Staying with a task was for once not a problem for my son. He knew that, as soon as a large enough part of the yard was cleared, his kite would be high in the sky. An hour or so later, I tucked the molded plastic spindle handle into a fat, mittened hand and shouted "Run!"

With Olympian determination he shot across the back lawn, going about as fast as a four-year-old with thirty pounds of clothes on can go. But it was fast enough. With each step the kite looped its way higher until it found its spot above the house where it "locked in."

I was amazed. The kite did not move but held high and steady, barely shivering in the stiff, March wind.

My son squealed with delight, unable to appreciate how easy the process had been. "I got it, Dad," he insisted. "You don't have to worry. I got it."

Well, it was clear he did, so I went back to work. For the next hour, with only a few interruptions to wind in a little string or launch the kite again, I worked, tossing branches into a burning pile on the edge of the driveway.

In the late afternoon, when the wind died down, the kite lay in the yard, the lawn was clean, and the pile had grown as tall as my shoulders, tightly packed and eight feet across. I found a gallon of kerosene in the garage and emptied it evenly over the pile.

My son was busy winding the string back around the plastic handle. He was employing a preschool precision that insured this kite would never see above twelve feet again.

"Hey, buddy," I called, "put the string down and come here; I want to show you something."

When he was seated on the frozen ground and well back from danger, I recited our familiar family speech about matches. I tossed one on the pile, which whooshed into flame. For a full hour we sat on the ground, my arms wrapped around the child cuddled between my knees. Several times we moved farther back to protect our faces, which were by now toasty red from the heat of the white flame.

Like fathers and sons of ages long past, we gazed into waves of liquidy heat and surrendered to the warm hypnosis. While the twigs popped and limbs exploded in a spray of sparks, we stared as layer after layer of branches collapsed into a bed of shimmering, white coal.

"Look how pretty it is, Dad," he muttered. "Look at the colors!"

"It sure is," I said, shading his tender skin with my hand. "It looks so beautiful, but it's so dangerous. Even I have to always be very careful with fire, and I'm a grown-up."

"Oh, I'll always be very careful too, Dad," he said, sounding as serious as he could. "You don't ever have to worry about that."

As we sat wrapped together for long, quiet moments, I was aware that this was one of those rare shared times that both my son and I would remember.

The tapping on the kitchen window broke the spell. We turned to see my wife bouncing our T-shirted toddler, both of them smiling and waving as if to say, "We're having fun, too, just watching you guys!"

By now our bonfire was an amoeba-shaped pallet of smooth white coal, still radiating enough heat to turn us away at six feet.

"Oh! You know what?" I said. "I almost forgot that big limb from the maple behind the garage. I'll be right back. You stay away from the fire now."

As it turned out, the limb was still partially connected to the tree and required a little twisting to break it off. Hoisting the thickest part up on my hip, I hauled the limb around the garage. With surprise, I noticed the kite shooting straight up. My son, with the plastic handle back in his mitten, was running across the lawn.

"Dad, look!" he squealed. "Quick, look! I did it again!"

My encouraging cheer was choked in horror as I watched my jubilant child, with his head back, eyes on the kite, stumble right toward the fire.

I dropped the branch and ran with a sickening lethargy. "No! Stop!"

But it was too late. With his bare skin turned away from the fire, he passed through the warning wave of heat. Spinning awkwardly, he fell hands down on the white coals. The yellow plastic handle disappeared in a drip of blue fire, and his mittens burst into yellow flame.

In one reflexive, inexplicable motion, his body bounced off the fire and back on his feet. As his mother shot through the front door and I raced toward my boy, I saw in his face a numb confusion that tore at my memory. Almost with indifference he watched black smoke pouring from his hands.

Within minutes his arms were wrapped in ice, the emergency room had been called, and we were on our way to the hospital.

"Oh, Dad, it hurts so bad," he said through his sobs. "Oh, please, can't you help me? I can't stand it."

At that moment, as I slowed for even the smallest bumps, my father's words from long ago became prophetic: "Someday, Bob, you'll understand."

With a heart so full of love I thought it would break, I heard myself say the words, and more honest words I'd never spoken. "Son, if I could, I would take the pain in your hands and put it right into my own."

"Oh, no, Dad," he said, unable to wipe his own tears. "You don't know how bad this hurts."

"It doesn't matter, son. If I could, I'd take it all."

I am thankful to say that years later the only physical reminder of this incident is a crumpled ointment tube in the medicine cabinet. But the effect on me was permanent.

From my earliest memories, I had felt God's merciful arms embrace me and His loving hand shield my face from the fire. All my life, I had rested in His warm grace and beheld the hypnotic beauty of His creation. I had listened to His words and been comforted by His teaching.

But carelessly, I had avoided the awesome magnitude of His love and pain. With my face turned away and my eyes on the world, I stumbled through life oblivious to His choking cries of warning.

Now, through my child, I began to understand. At least I understood enough to be able to ask, "Can it really be, God? Can it really be that long ago, on Calvary's tree, You bore my sin in Your body?"

The question scorched my heart, and I screamed, "No, God, You don't want to do that! It's too much! I won't let You! Can it really be, God, that You have taken all my suffering and left me without a scar?"

Through shameful tears that I am unable to dry myself, I heard God's words of assurance. From a heart so full of love that it was broken for me, God said, "I have cleansed you from all your unrighteousness through Jesus Christ your Lord." More honest words were never spoken.

CHAPTER FIVE

YOU KNOW WHEN YOU DON'T BELONG

T ake your pick," I said. "We can go wherever you want."
Spread before my wife and me, covering about half the floor in our tiny basement apartment, was a map of the United States.

Judy responded with mock confusion. "I'm sorry; I don't understand. I'm looking for Paris, but I can't seem to find it."

We had spent nearly two years of marriage living in three rooms. I had been working for a children's theater in Chicago, through a government grant, trying to get any experience I could. Judy was graduating from college in the spring, after which we planned to move. We weren't yet sure where we were going, but we planned to be on our way by mid-May.

The first round of "pin the tale on the homeland" put us in Massachusetts. The second round put us in the Berkshires, an ideal place to begin my work. We didn't know it at the time, but it was also an ideal place for Judy to begin hers.

While I was following road maps all over southern New England, knocking on doors, passing out brochures filled with good things I'd written about myself, trying to get performances anywhere I could, Judy's vocation was dumped on her.

One day the phone rang. Someone wanted information about shows. Judy answered a few questions as best she could and said she would send out some materials "right away." The phone has never stopped ringing to this day, and Judy has never stopped answering it and sending out materials right away. She became an agent by answering one phone call.

I thought this was a wonderful thing. She didn't even have to go for a job interview. And she was a natural. People began to express disappointment when I arrived for shows without my wife. Efficiency is her first and middle name, and her commission went right into our bank account. What could be better?

"Well, for starters," she informed me, "it would be better if I had a job I wanted to do, not one I have to do because there's no one else around to do it."

If our children had not come along when they did, I might have had to knock on more doors to try to find someone else to answer my phone and send things out right away. But with babies in the next room and my income always an "act of God," Judy's enthusiasm about her "work" seemed to grow.

She would say things like "You know, I think I probably just have to resign myself to doing this for a while" or "I know it's a big help. I'm the logical one to do it, and it just seems to be the best thing."

Of course, things are not always what they "just seem to be." Researchers in parapsychology might be interested to learn that when babies are screaming and toddlers are toddling, telephones know all about it. I realized Judy was trying to hold down two jobs that really didn't complement each other.

The situation was comparable to a pastor counseling the bereaved while officiating "All-Star Wrestling." Neither party is going to get the attention he or she deserves, and someone could get killed. We needed to find a solution.

One late afternoon I returned from a long day on the road. I had just begun my "daddy duties," lying face down on the living room rug while the boys took turns jumping on my back, when the phone rang. One look toward Judy told me I would be wise to answer it. The call was from California.

"You don't know me," said a very young man's voice, "but I saw you perform several years ago at my university. I thought you were great. I'm wondering if you're still at it."

"Just as much as I can be," I replied, as my youngest flew through the air and stuck to my thigh. "Are you looking for some entertainment?"

"Well, no," he said, sounding a little less young. "Actually, I'm looking for a client."

Three days later, Judy and I dressed up, left the kids with a sitter and headed for town. We were both nervous. What an answer to prayer! The young man was an associate in perhaps the most reputable booking agency in my field of entertainment. He had been ordered by his superiors to bring in a new act, and he had chosen me!

"We're going to need to pull together some new promo and have glossies shot, which may require a few minor image alterations," he had said. "I can fly in on Saturday if you and your wife would like to meet me for dinner. It'll be on me. Are you available?"

"I don't know," I said. "Let me check."

A glance at my calendar confirmed my suspicion. I was pretty much available through the beginning of the next century. "Yeah,"

I said, "I think I can juggle some things around."

"Can you make reservations someplace nice?"

"How nice?" I asked.

"Can you find us someplace very nice?" he toyed.

"I sure can," I said.

And I sure did. We were heading for unquestionably the finest eating establishment in southern New England.

The restaurant itself was a little intimidating. (I knew I should have polished my loafers.)

And there wasn't one man awaiting us for dinner; there were three. Two of them had no idea who I was or what I did. The young man I'd spoken to on the phone was identifiably the junior partner and behaved as if his tenure would be determined during the meal.

The boss, the one with the most jewelry, kept looking at his watch as my new little agent talked on and on, trying to describe in detail portions of my show remembered from five years earlier. Portions of my show I didn't even remember. Portions of my show he obviously felt forced to embellish, laughing all by himself, wiping questionable tears from behind his horned rims. Finally he'd say, "Well, I guess you had to be there."

The third man placed before me an agency press packet. "This is the kind of treatment we'd like to suggest," he said, almost smiling.

I opened a high-gloss, logo-embossed folder that displayed 8×10's of their top performers. Most were bare chested, with pectoral-length, curly perms and V-shaped guitars. Several had lightning shooting out of the tops of their heads. I felt a painful rush of embarrassment.

I glanced at Judy, who was thoughtfully perusing the photos, trying to smile pleasantly, almost disguising that she had begun doing natural childbirth rhythmic breathing exercises.

The rest of the evening is a bit of a blur. I remember sweating a lot and feeling I didn't belong there. Not in that restaurant. Not with those people. Not in that press packet.

You know when you don't belong. I should have spoken up right then. I should have said, "Hey, listen, I'm sorry—sorry you flew out and wasted your time and money, but this will never work. I just don't belong in your agency."

But I didn't speak up in time. Papers were passed across the table, and I signed my name.

As I recall that evening, I'm reminded of a similar, earlier experience. I was an eighth-grader in my best suit at the big dance with my seventh-grade sweetheart. It could have been a great memory except for one thing.

I didn't belong there, either. This wasn't a junior high event. This was the Freshmen Frolic for senior high students only.

So what were we doing there? Well, I just didn't speak up in time.

I had finished singing in the district junior high chorale in a nearby town. That's why I was dressed up. I had asked my mom to drop me off at the high school so I could look in the gym's door to see the decorations.

People did that sort of thing in my little town. Moms and dads and younger children would look in the door, listen to the music and try to make out the pretty shapes in gowns and tuxes. It was an event, and even if you didn't belong inside, it was all right to look in the door and imagine the future or remember the past.

When I walked in the lobby, there she was. She was sort of my girlfriend. Beautiful in her white district chorale gown, with her red hair and freckles, she was the kind of skinny girl older boys would look at and say, "She's going to be a knockout some day." But I thought she was a knockout right now. And there she was by herself in her formal gown, looking in the door. And here I was in my best and only suit, standing next to her and thinking how nice it would be when we were old enough to belong inside.

I spotted two of my freshmen buddies just about the time they spotted me. With their dates on their arms, they made their way glowing past rows of black lights, illuminating the giant chicken wire and Kleenex Moby Dick.

"Hey, Bob, are you guys actually coming in? I can't believe it! You're all dressed up. You're actually coming in, aren't you?"

"No," I said, "we were at district chorale. We were just—"

"Hey, listen," said one of the ravishing dates. "Mr. Bates is taking tickets. He probably won't even notice you're in junior high."

"Yeah," said another, getting excited about the idea. "It's dark in there. He can hardly see as it is. I think you could pull this off."

"No, no," I said. "We weren't coming in. We were just at district—"

My closest buddy in the bunch interrupted me. "Listen!" he counseled, "if Bates sells you a ticket, you're not doing anything wrong! Right? I mean, if you've got the money, which I'd be happy to loan you, and if you're dressed properly, which you almost are, and if you've got a date, which you do, and if Mr. Bates sells you a ticket— then what's the problem?"

I should have said, "Hey, listen. I'm sorry—sorry to let you down, but this won't work. We don't belong in there." But I didn't speak up in time.

Next thing I knew, we were through the gymnasium door, standing before old Mr. Bates, who was all dressed up like a sea horse.

I was praying, "Please, God, don't let him sell me the tickets."

I wanted to scream, "Mr. Bates, it's me, Bobby Stromberg. I used to mow your lawn. I'm still a kid. I just sang first alto in district chorale. Look at this girl I'm with. Can't you see the difference? We don't belong here. You're our last chance. *Please, Mr. Bates, look at us!*"

To my relief, he did. He stopped and looked me right in my eyes. A little smile came over his lips. He handed me the tickets and said, "Have a wonderful evening, young man."

My older buddies let out a whoop, and we were through the octopus' mouth and onto the deck of Ahab's ship. I felt faint. My chest was pounding right along with the beat of Ollie and the Heart Throbs. I thought I was going to be seasick. We would be caught. We were stowaways. It didn't matter that we paid our fare. We didn't belong, and someone would notice we weren't old enough to be on board. And what about the sharks, the chaperons and the school principal, swimming around out there? They'd smell us out.

Then, to my horror, I realized my "date" shared none of my fear. That little dip didn't even realize anything was wrong. She was pulling me into the sea of dancers. I was trying to get back on the deck and out the octopus' mouth.

The spotlight from the crow's nest searched the sea floor, coming toward us. I dove on my face, hiding under waves of fog from a dry ice machine. I wanted to drown at that point. It seemed a better alternative than the death I would suffer when my parents found out where I had been. And the sharks! I knew they were coming now.

The band pounded on,

"I said a no, no, no, it ain't me, babe.

It ain't me you're lookin' for, babe."

I crawled through what seemed like thousands of dancing high heels and patent leather rental shoes, trying to avoid the oxblood wing tips of the Great White. Then I was under the ship's stern, through some chicken wire and out a locker-room door into the cool, spring air.

I briefly thought about diving back in to save my sweetheart, poor thing. But then I figured that by now she was undoubtedly in the lobby, crying and complaining to the school principal that she had a ticket just like everyone else. She would fail to understand what had just happened. Fail to understand that we had not belonged.

I walked back home, my shirt soaked through, my socks almost squishing in my shoes. But I was alive and back where I belonged, hoping never to make that mistake again.

Now here I was, nearly twenty years later, eating seafood with some big shots from the coast.

"Help us with this, Bob," said the boss, the one with the most rows of teeth. "We need a line for the brochure. Complete this sentence. An evening with Bob Stromberg is like . . . What can you give us? What do we need? What do you hear?"

"Well, I don't know," I said. "I've never really thought . . . I mean it's difficult to . . ."

"Just let it flow," said the third man, coaxing with both arms.

"Well," I stammered, "really, ah, you . . . I suppose . . . in a way . . . mostly I . . ."

My young agent looked at me with despair, like a man about to walk the plank.

"Well," I said, "I guess an evening with Bob Stromberg is like family night at Bible camp."

My words had the stunning effect of a well placed harpoon. All sound was silenced. All movement ceased. Forks full of fish were frozen in mid-ascent. This Bermuda-Triangle suspension might have persisted had my pale, young agent not needed to excuse himself from the table.

The rest of us finished our meals and talked hopefully about our new relationship, which we inwardly knew could not last. One year later, at contract renewal time, the agency informed me that they were unable to profitably market my performance concept. All of us were undoubtedly relieved.

Judy, however, to her occasional frustration, continues to find the concept remarkably marketable. She just continues to serve people year after year. She answers the phone. She sends out materials, and she sends them out right away. I then follow behind and do what they've asked me to do.

This, of course, is a simplification of the process, but it's key to something wonderful in our lives—a sense of belonging.

Last spring, with our trees in blossom and our landscaping in full bloom, Judy and I sat in our beloved New England colonial home and looked at a map of the United States.

"Well," I said, "take your pick. We can go wherever you want."

Today we live as a family in an apartment on the north side of Chicago. It has not been an easy adjustment for any of us. It seems at times the sudden cultural contrasts will fracture our souls. But beneath, supported by past experience and the promise of God, there persists a wonderful assurance in our lives. We belong.

CHAPTER SIX

MIRACLE AT STINKY BAY

I remember when I was eight years old, my father told my mother and my sister and me that we were going over to my Aunt Martha and Uncle Glen's to say good-bye and to wish them a great trip and to tell them to catch a batch of big ones for us.

It was a beautiful summer evening. The weatherman said there were many more on the way, and at four o'clock in the morning the very next day, my aunt and uncle were leavin' to fish in Canada. (Northern Ontario, to be precise—the only place to catch the really big ones.)

My uncle would say, "Why, the biggest fish we catch around here, up there we'd just throw away." And then he'd said, "If a fish is twelve inches, maybe thirteen, ahhh, throw it back in; it isn't even big enough to clean."

My uncle took out a tackle box that looked to me like a chest of precious treasure, filled with shiny new fishing lures and some rusty old faithfuls thrown in for good measure. There were red rubber

mice and gummy green worms that didn't look particularly realis-
tic to me, but apparently a hungry pike isn't so apt to see those
enormous hooks, and before he knows it . . . Wham! . . . he's
posin' for the camera with my aunt and uncle, who are smilin' just
as big as they're able. And later my cousins and I are starin' at
those pictures on the picnic table.

Now the fishin' lures that looked like real fish, well, they were
bigger than any real fish I'd ever caught, with names like the Bass
Buster and the Walleyed Wonder. Then my uncle would reach
beneath the bottom tray and lift out a lure that made me stare
in awe.

"This one, son," he'd say, "this one's to catch the king of 'em all."

I looked at a picture on the package that looked like a monster
and at the words, "Muskie Maul."

"Ohhhh, these fish are big, son," my uncle would say, raising
his eyebrow in a menacing way. "And mean! Why, they'll take
your finger clean off to the top knuckle."

My father put his hand on my shoulder and chuckled at my
uncle. "Yeah, Glen? Well, you've got ten days to bring home the
proof. We'll be waitin'."

And so we were. Ten days later they drove in the drive, hand-
shakin' and hugs all around. Then my uncle took three big ice
chests out of the trunk and clunked them down on the ground. He
opened them up. One . . . two . . . three.

No one made a sound. No one could, except to breathe a little
quicker.

There must have been fifty shinin' fish: two monster muskies,
six northern pike, pickerel, perch, walleye and catfish (both large
mouth and small). All of them more than two feet long. One
northern was nearly three feet. The others were close to four. And
both muskies were six or seven inches more.

"Next year you gotta come," my uncle said. "Why, you should have seen the ones that got away! You see that bass right there? It jumped in the boat all by itself the day before yesterday. Oh, and look it here!" He laid a pike across my forearms, all frozen and smelly. "Look it here!" he said, pointing at the fish, "I snagged that one right in the belly."

My father just smiled and sighed, but I could see fish fever in his eyes. Yes, my dad was hooked like a chinook through the gills. Before even one of those fish was grilled and eaten, he had called a meetin' with Uncle Glen and some other men he thought might like to go the following summer.

As the year progressed, I saw the plans come together. But I'd heard no thoughts concerning me, whether I'd be allowed to go.

Finally in February my father spoke to me following an evening meal. "This summer you'll be nine. And your mom and I feel that's old enough, though it's gonna be tough at times. It won't be easy. We'll be up early in the mornin'. We'll probably fish till late at night—you gotta fish while the fish bite, son. But if you think you can make it . . . well, I'd love for you to come along."

And so I did. We drove all night, so it didn't seem too far. At least it didn't seem so to me, curled up sleepin' in the back of the car. We drove through a forest at sunrise and then over a stream and parked the car right alongside it, where we were met by two young men in canoes. They were sent to guide us to our camp cottages and their wilderness home where we'd eat enormous breakfasts and dinners prepared by their mother, Ruby. We knew her to be one of the best cooks in northern Canada.

I remember that first night we gathered 'round a kerosene lamp on a card table and looked at some maps of mostly water and some trails that would enable us to portage (canoes and boats on our backs) from one lake to the next. The men drank some coffee. I had some cocoa.

Then my dad and I turned in early so we would be able to rise with the loons.

And that's what we did. The next day we fished from early mornin' till late at night, and I don't think I had even one, single bite. Oh, once I thought I did, but it turned out to be some roots from an old lily pad, and I was really disappointed.

But not my dad. He said, "Hey, tomorrow's another day. We'll get 'em!"

But we didn't—not that day, and not the next day, either. We were three days into a seven-day trip, and except for my uncle, who snagged a beaver, we'd caught zip. Oh, I got a few little perch, and my dad caught a couple of bony trout, but they were nothing to write home to Mom about.

That night we gathered 'round the kerosene lamp again, and frankly, I don't think any of the men were happy with my Uncle Glen.

He said, "Okay, listen. I think tomorrow maybe we ought to stay right here and fish Clear Lake."

The others said, "Fine. Good."

But my father said, "I think I'll take Bobby out through this wood and see if we can find Stinky Bay."

The others said, "Fine. Okay. It's probably better we split up anyway."

So the next day we left at sunrise. Dad was in the back and I in the bow, with plenty of bait, rods, reels and an additional small motor my dad could shoulder overland into Stinky Bay. There the guide had agreed to leave us another small boat and a can of gas just past a stand of pines.

We traveled half an hour over water, twice that overland, and by eight o'clock (just about the time I thought my legs would give out), we crested a knoll, and down through a hole in the leaves, we saw the morning sun reflecting on our destination. It really wasn't a bay at all, but more like a pond full of lily pads and other vegetation. It was about twice the size of the green in our town square. It looked as though it was full of fish, and my dad and I were the only fishermen there.

At 8:15 we threw in our first bobbers to float, and at 8:16 we had two big bass floppin' in the bottom of the boat. We couldn't believe it.

We didn't even have to change our bait. Everything we threw in they ate. Wham, pickerel! Wham, perch. Wham, crappy, catfish, bass! Big and mean, everyone put up a fight.

We knew we'd never be able to carry them all out if we fished till night, so we decided to keep only the best. The rest we let go, even though we knew the other men would never know, nor believe, we'd caught so many.

By noon we had the most beautiful selection of fish you could take from a Canadian lake, with the exception of the monster muskie. Each fight was a thrill, after which we'd hook the fish through the gill on a stringer and toss it back in over the side of the boat, floating securely alongside.

About one o'clock, the hot sun began to slow things down a bit, so we ate our lunches from our sacks. We then threw our lines for another hour or so, until my dad said, "You know, we've done so well, maybe we ought to go."

My nose had begun to burn pretty bad. And I had been up since five in the morning, so agreein' with my dad, I reached for the stringer. But the stringer wasn't there.

My father said, "Well, when did you see it last?"

"I don't know."

"What did you move it for?"

"I didn't move it!" I said. "Maybe you did when you were lookin' for lunch."

But it didn't matter who did what, because the stringer was gone right over the side. Somewhere in that deep water, down among those lily pads, twenty fish swam unusually close, nearly nose to nose, in fact, connected by a metal stringer through the gills, and all our thrills were for nothing.

For the next hour, Dad and I took turns rowing, while the other searched the deep waters for a flash of fish, a shine of metal, a glimmer, a glimpse—anything to give us hope. But no, the stringer was gone right over the side.

Dad just sort of sat and stared. And I cried some, I admit it. And I prayed quietly, "Oh, God, could You help us get it, so we can show Uncle Glen and the other men? And if You do, I'll thank You. I'll give You my allowance. I'll be a missionary!"

But the stringer was gone right over the side.

Dad said, "Hey, it's not that bad. We can fish a while. Maybe we'll catch a few."

But that's not what I wanted to do, and besides Dad and I knew we'd never be able to catch a batch like we did before. So finally, depressed, we started in to shore.

I threw in my hook with a little toss. Maybe a miracle muskie from God would make up for the loss. But no, the hook just got hung up on a lily pad.

So my dad had to row back as I reeled in until I could reach over to release the hook. But it wouldn't come. The harder I pulled, the tighter it got until finally I had such a terrible mess of line and knots I said, "Dad, why don't you just cut the line? It's just a fifty cent plug."

But he decided he wanted to give it a tug, which he did. His muscles were taut, and the line cut into his fingers until *pop*! went the line, and up came the stringer! Up came a stringer of beautiful fish, caught on my line, wrapped around the root! We let out a hoot you could have heard for miles around.

My prayers had come true. And then it seemed the only right thing to do was to thank God, which we did with grateful hearts.

Oh, my Uncle Glen and the other men would never believe. And my friends, when I told them, would just laugh right in my face. But it didn't matter, because I would always remember that pond as a holy place. Something special had happened that day. It was, as my dad and I say, the miracle at Stinky Bay.

CHAPTER SEVEN

THE
BEE BAGGER

A s I tell this story, I have before me two common objects that have had great significance in my life. The first is my accordion, and the second is a vacuum cleaner now belonging to my wife.

The accordion made me famous. It made my name a household word throughout McKean County. And this vacuum cleaner won me a genuine leather-bound certificate of recognition when I was only eleven years old. Let me read the certificate to you:

> Presented by the town council to young Robert Stromberg, Jr., in recognition of his efforts and success in saving the annual canoe race, and yes, this whole town of Canoe Place, from economic disaster.

> Rev. Earnest Swanson   Harold T. Myer
> Pastor of the Community Church   Mayor
> and Town Treasurer   July 11, 1963

So you see, this accordion and this vacuum have made me what I am today. How could my life be changed by things like these?

The answer is bees! That's right, bees!

I grew up in northwestern Pennsylvania. Springtime was wonderful. Summers were hot but bearable. Autumns were beautiful beyond belief. But the winters were terrible—cold, lots of snow. But you know, the snow is the lifeblood of my old town.

In the spring the snow melts and flows down off the hills. And it falls into the creeks and streams and fills the headwaters of the Allegheny River. Long ago Indians paddled canoes of birch bark here, searching for a place to park. A sandy spot, good and wide, with plenty of space. And that's how my town got its name, Canoe Place.

Every year for generations, my town has had an annual riverfront celebration to remember its beginnings. The main event was a canoe race with sizable winnings for the victors. So racers came from all over the state to test their strength, skill and fate. From Turtle Point through Burning Bush, every joint and muscle of every contender pushed to be the first past Deerlick Ridge and across the finish line at the Mill Street Bridge. A thousand people cheered on the riverbank, including Mayor Harold T. Myer (most called him Hank), who stayed and congratulated every person who participated in making the river race the pride that it was.

Then the fun really began. Parents followed as children ran to the town square to buy tickets for the pony rides. Everybody brought food, and being in the mood to celebrate, they ate and ate and spent a lot of money on homemade fudge, honey and fruit jams. The town ladies sold cookbooks, and the firemen sold barbecued chicken breasts. The farmers sold onions and leeks. And there was no more room in the Canoe Place Inn for the whole week.

Yes, to all it was clear. The Canoe Place Race was the most important event in town year after year after year. And people began to wonder, "If we couldn't have the race, would the town go under? I mean, what would we do? And heavens, what if we missed two summers?" That had never happened to date.

There was, of course, the drought of '38, the year summer came too soon. That's right. It wouldn't wait till June. It started in mid-April, ninety degrees. Why, by the middle of May, you could walk right across the deepest spot in the river and not even dampen your knees. But the summer of '39 was a beauty!

Then there was the tornado of '62. Did what twisters usually do— tore up half the town. No race that year. But folks said, "Yeah, well it's hard, but next summer things will turn around."

But the summer of '63, it looked as if things might not turn around.

I first became aware of the problem midspring. I went out in the yard barefoot and got a bee sting right on my toe. It hurt like the dickens.

But that was nothing compared to David Kanally's pain. He was licking on a sucker and was stung right on his puckerer. It swelled up really big.

Not as big as Mrs. Huff, however. She was stung on her finger, and her whole body puffed up. Well, David couldn't smile very well for a while, and I cried, but poor Mrs. Huff almost died.

Then the newspaper guys started to report stings all over town. Soon other town papers picked up the story, and then Mayor Myer started to worry.

"Three weeks until the festival and canoe race," he mumbled, a continuous sound, "and no one is going to come if we can't chase these bees out of town."

They tried to blame my Uncle Carl. He kept bees in little, white, stacked houses out in the fields at his farm.

But he said, "My bees have done no one any harm, so all of you guys just wait. My bees got forty acres of flowered fields to pollinate. You think they're going to fly five miles into town?"

Most argued my uncle was probably right. So the very next night the town council flew in a biological research team from Buffalo. They studied the situation for a week or so and then presented their findings at a special town forum. Mayor Myer presided.

"We have determined that we have a quorum, that is clear. In fact, it looks like the whole town is here. Now, Dr. Distachio from Buffalo, we wait upon you for your report."

Dr. Distachio, distinguished for his studies of bees and fleas and other haplodapoids, said the sting reports surely were true.

"We ourselves have been annoyed," he said, displaying a sting on the front of his head. "The problem is clear."

People sat up.

"You've got too many bees around here. The solution . . ."

People leaned forward to listen.

"We have determined, the bees must be exterminated. The method . . ."

Eyes stared, wide open.

"As best we can tell, wait until the autumn, when the warm weather dies, and the bees will as well. Thank you. So glad we could be of service." And he nervously grabbed his notes and shot for the door.

People shouted, "Wait a minute. You've told us nothing we didn't know before."

"Order!" shouted Mayor Myer, banging his gavel on the table. "I hereby declare a one-hundred-dollar reward to anyone able to rid our town of this plague. And we've got only a week to do it!"

People left discouraged, for no one had a clue how it could be done. Of all those people, I was certainly one.

* * *

The solution I found, I found by mistake. I was practicing this old accordion, the accordion that made me famous, that made my name a household word throughout McKean County.

This old accordion, however, was not the one I wanted. The one I wanted stood in the music store window, where I looked at it everyday after school. One hundred twenty buttons, fifty-three keys, red sparkle plastic with white bellows, and three sound bars for harmonica, violins and cellos. And the bellows had no holes, so they didn't wheeze on every squeeze.

Oh, I wanted it badly. But it cost more money than I had, you see. It cost one hundred fifty bucks. Well, I'd thought of every possible way to earn some money, but shucks, a hundred fifty bucks was almost inconceivable.

Now, what I'm going to tell you is true, though I know it sounds unbelievable. I was practicing this old accordion, given to me by my grandpa, when I realized something was just not right.

"Mom," I cried, "there's something wrong with these keys."

My mom stuck her head in the door. "Maybe you should read the notes on the page. We've been through this before."

"I know," I protested, "but this time that's not the problem. I can't even get any air out of it."

I struggled against the plugged bellows. "This makes me so mad!"

Then a bee came out of the air hole. And then another and another and another.

I screamed to my mother, "Mom, there are bees in my bedroom!" and threw the accordion on the floor.

Through a crack in the door my mom and I watched eighty-four bees leave the bellows. Then eighty-five.

"I've about had it. Sakes alive," Mom said, anger in her face. "These bees have gone too far. You see if you can get that accordion in its case; I'll go start the car."

Soon we were riding down the road to my grandma and grandpa's. We found them in Grandpa's workshop down in the cellar.

Grandpa said, "Well, there's my big fella! Bobby, how are you doing?"

"Not so good, Grandpa," I said. "I think your accordion is ruined."

He was working on Grandma's old vacuum cleaner. My grandma looked about as unhappy as I'd ever seen her.

"Well," my grandpa said, "this seems to be the day for things to break down."

He had the vacuum cleaner all opened up so you could see the gears spinning around. "I think this old cleaner is finally dead. You can only fix something so many times before it's gone for good.

"I'd buy that new one down at Meacham's Hardware, if I could. It's what they call an Electrolux. But I'd have to pay out a hundred fifty bucks for the thing, and that's about a hundred fifty bucks more than I could swing right now. That makes the housework kind of tough for your grandma, you know. This old guy still pulls a little. Not enough, though."

My grandma said, "I guess that means it's back to a dust pan and broom for me. Though that's not going to help much in the dining room or on the rug by the TV."

My grandma worked hard as it was. But without a vacuum cleaner, she'd have to work even harder, because it was a big house.

"Grandpa," I said, "I feel really bad about your accordion. It was only a couple of days I didn't play it, but that's all it took. A bunch of bees came in and made it their home. For all I know, a big old honeycomb is inside. I mean it, Grandpa; I didn't practice for just a couple of days; that's all it took."

"Well, Bobby," Grandpa said, "put her up here on the bench, and we'll take a look."

He popped off the front first and looked in behind the keys. "Nope, Bobby, no bees."

"Play something, Grandpa."

My grandpa gave it a squeeze.

About halfway through the second line of "My Wild Irish Rose," those bees started coming out the hole right in front of my nose. Not caring for that particular song, they were mad. My grandpa was into the song by now, and squeezing with all his strength, he was completely unaware the bees were even there.

I can't tell you exactly why I did it, but I saw the button for the vacuum cleaner, reached down and hit it. It fired up. Some bees by now were trying to get back in by the hole, sort of hovering around. I put the nozzle by the hole, and the vacuum sucked them right down, slick as could be. All the other bees trying to get out or in had to pass by me, and I bagged 'em. Sucked 'em right down the tube.

My grandpa finally stopped and said, "I think it just needs a little lubricating; be fine as the day I bought it."

I could hear the bees inside the cleaner bag, buzzing, meaner now than they ought to have been, seeing how it was my accordion they'd been living in.

"Grandpa, do you mind if I borrow this vacuum for a week or so?"

"My goodness no," he said. "In fact, you can have it, if you want. Won't do you much good, though. Suction's almost gone. I'd buy that new one down at Meacham's Hardware, if I could. What they call an Electrolux . . ." And then my grandpa told me the story all over again.

***

The first thing I had to do was get rid of the bees in the bag. My uncle had all those bees in the little, white, stacked houses out in his field, so he had a special suit, netting and helmet to shield him from stings.

I tied the vacuum on my bike basket with some old strings and bungy straps and started to ride the five miles out into the country.

My mind was racing as fast as my feet could go. I imagined that new accordion in the music store window, with one hundred twenty buttons, fifty-three keys, red sparkle plastic with white bellows and three sound bars for harmonica, violins and cellos. And the bellows had no holes, so they didn't wheeze on every squeeze.

I could buy it if I could get rid of the bees in town and win the reward. I could bag the bees and solve the puzzle that had alluded all the town's wise adults from Mayor Myer on down. The bees would be gone, and I could say I did what I did 'cause the canoe race must go on. People would cheer. And I would take my check for one hundred bucks, and with some other money I'd earn, with any luck, I'd buy that accordion.

My uncle said my plan might just work. The bees I'd bagged were big ones, might make a lot of honey. Furthermore, he'd give me a buck a bag—some of the money I needed to make the extra fifty dollars.

"Bobby, if I had to bet," my uncle said, "I'd say there's probably no more than a dozen big nests you have to get. They might be in trees, though bees will build in a stone wall, under the eaves or in an old junk car. All you have to do is search the town near and far with a fine-tooth comb. Find out where those bees have built their homes. You're going to need extra bags for that old vacuum. I have a box of them in the shed."

My uncle leaned against a fence post and scratched his head. "You only have six days till the race. Mayor Myer has talked to the newsmen, and the editor has agreed that what Canoe Place doesn't need is more people hearing about bees. So, more than likely, people will be here on race day. The question is, will the bees chase them all away."

He shook his head. "The answer is no. Not if you can do your job, Bobby! Now I suggest you take tomorrow, get on your bike and find those nests. Remember, you're only looking for the five or six best."

He started to walk toward the shed. "Now, you know there's one by Mrs. Huff's, and she's in the hospital yet, so it won't be too tough to plug right into her patio outlet.

"Once you find the five you think are the biggest, get up before sunrise. Get the nozzle right by the hole where you've seen them coming and going. When they go for their morning stroll, you bag 'em.

"Now, there might be a thousand bees in one hive, so you're going to have to keep going most of the day. Put some rocks on the nozzle, or stick it to a wall with tape so the nozzle doesn't fall and let the bees escape. That way you can empty a couple of nests a day. By the weekend, the town should be okay."

Uncle Carl reached into his shed of bee-keeping equipment and pulled out some netting. "Stick this under your hat," he said, "and wear gloves and long pants, and remember that time's running out! Good luck, son."

I spent Sunday afternoon riding up one street and down another, asking every child and father and mother, "Have you seen any nests? Any problem with bees?"

I crawled under porches and climbed up in trees. By nightfall I knew where I had to go. Eight big nests. I'd have time for only five or six, though, at best.

I had a toy helmet I got in third grade, and I stuck a big bumblebee I made on it. I had some black jeans and a sweatshirt the same. On my shirt, helmet and bike frame, with big, yellow letters, I taped on "The Bee Bagger."

That evening I went down to Grandma and Grandpa's. My grandma had a long, yellow extension cord she said I could borrow. She said, "You want it for a week? Goodness, bring it back a month from tomorrow as far as I'm concerned. It doesn't much matter to me." She looked tired. "The only reason for having a cord that long was to plug in my vacuum, and now that that's gone, I'll never use it anyway."

Grandma opened the closet where she stored the cord. "Your grandfather says he'd buy us a new one tomorrow if we could afford it. But he did fix up this little sweeper."

She showed me the kind her mother used to use. It wasn't electric, so you couldn't blow a fuse, and you didn't have to plug it in. And it wasn't noisy, which was good. But, then again, it didn't do a great job like a new one would. I felt badly for Grandma, because she always worked hard.

When I left, I found my grandpa looking at the sign on my bike. "Bobby, have you got in mind what I think you might?"

"Yep," I said, "you got it, Grandpa. The bees will be gone by Friday night!"

Grandma looked confused, and my grandpa looked proud. As I rode off, I heard Grandpa laugh aloud.

***

That night I set my alarm for 4:15, because from all I had read and heard and seen, the bees wouldn't fly till the sun warmed the air. When the bees left the hive, I planned to be there. And so I was.

I rode to Mrs. Huff's through the cool morning fog and across her back lawn to a stone wall by a log. I found the hole I had watched the day before. It seemed a thousand bees, maybe more, were in the hive, though this morning there was no sign of them.

I plugged in Grandma's long, yellow extension cord and ran it from the patio outlet across the lawn to the hive. I hit the switch at ten minutes till five.

I turned it back off at 5:15 because not one bee had yet flown. The motor was tired and starting to moan. I stared at the hole for a full ninety minutes, and just when I thought there must be nothing in it, a bee poked out its nose.

"You must be looking for me, I suppose?" I asked.

The question was rhetorical. I hit the button, and the bee was historical.

Then one after another, too many to be numbered, the bees peeped out of the hole. I filled five bags while half the town still slumbered.

Then off on my buzzing bee cycle I flew, dropping the bags by my uncle's at 9:32. Then back on my bike I rode once again and peddled through town at ten after ten.

The Kanallys were all up in Canada fishin', so again I needed not ask permission. The nest was in a drain pipe that had filled up with leaves, so I taped the nozzle up under the eaves and plugged the cord in a box on the wall.

Most of the worker bees were already out. But when they came back, I bagged several thousand, or there about. That's another three bags back out to the farm. So far my plan worked like a charm!

Uncle Carl took the bees, paid me the money and then said, "Come and have some lunch."

We had peanut butter sandwiches with honey, saltine crackers with real butter, and fresh, cold milk from the cow.

My uncle said, "Bobby, tell me now, is the plan working well?"

"Yeah, Uncle Carl, so far the bees are behaving. The vacuum has just enough suction. Uncle Carl, I think I'm saving the town from economic destruction."

Then off I rode in the hot summer sun and was back in town at a quarter past one. I got permission to use a plug inside the home of old Mrs. Sturgic.

She said, "I haven't been out all summer for fear of the bees. I'm powerful allergic."

I cleaned out her hive in two and half hours. Just to make her feel safer, I vacuumed a few stray bees off her lawn and flowers.

That afternoon and evening, I sucked in another six bags of bees from the Andersons' porch ceiling and the Swansons' pear trees.

And Friday morning I finished off a hive in an old junker bus. People were noticing a difference.

"Why, doesn't the sky look blue?" folks said. "Doesn't your spirit feel lighter?"

I myself knew that, when I listened carefully, it did seem noticeably quieter.

***

Mayor Myer's phone stopped ringing, and he wondered, "Is it possible the bees have stopped stinging?"

"Well, nobody knows," said one commissioner.

"Could be. I suppose," said a selectman.

Lawrence Ritter, who wrote for the newspaper, was out on the street doing interviews, asking folks what they thought about the miracle, about the exodus of bees.

Folks were saying, "Yep, really something. Hard to understand."

And then Ritter ran into my grandpa, who said, "Now listen to me, young man, I know the how, and I know the who! You tell Mayor Myer now, he better do what he said he'd do!" And my grandpa told the reporter the whole story.

Mr. Ritter said, "Don't you worry. I'll tell the mayor. Now, where is the boy?"

I was bagging my last big nest, probably twice the size of all the rest. I was hanging by my knees in one of the town square maple trees, when the flash bulbs started popping. I looked down to see Mr. Ritter, several other reporters and, to my amazement, Mayor Myer himself!

"Son, that's ingenious!" he said. "Where'd you ever get an idea like that?"

Then I told him the whole story like I just told you.

"If the people come this weekend," the mayor said, "and if they stay, I hereby swear that I shall declare 'Bobby the Bee Bagger Day.'

We'll have a town-wide celebration, at which time you shall receive your just reward."

The annual Riverfront Celebration was a great success. And yes, a few people did get stung, but no more than had ever been stung before.

So the following Saturday, across the main street of the town, a big banner was strung. And when numerous speeches were spoken and anthems were sung, I was presented my plaque, through thunderous applause, and a one-hundred-dollar bill.

Later that night I dug down in my drawer full of sox and dumped dollar bills on my bed from the old cigar box my grandpa had given me. With money I earned from my uncle for bagging the bees, and a few dollars I had from some other stuff, plus the hundred dollars I'd won, I figured I had just enough.

So Monday morning, with my head held high, a big smile on my face and lots of money in my wallet, I walked to town, where I looked through the store window. There it was. Though there were several, I'm sure everyone knows it was the one with the red sparkle finish that I quickly chose.

The salesman said, "You're buying a beauty when you buy one of these. Yes, you can even hear the quality. Never a rattle. Never a wheeze."

I gave him the money and said, "Wrap it up, please. Oh, and can you use some real pretty paper, and do you have a fancy bow?"

Now you might ask, "Why would you wrap it up with fancy paper and a bow?"

Clearly the reason is found in something you may not yet know. You see, I'd wanted that new accordion from the very first I'd seen her. But I didn't buy the new accordion. No, I bought a new vacuum cleaner. And when my grandparents opened that box and the tears came to their eyes, my heart was so happy, even I was surprised.

I learned something. To do something well and get paid for your part, that's good, and we should expect no less. But to do something simply out of the kindness of your heart, when the payment is just joy . . . now that's the very best.

CHAPTER EIGHT

DECEPTION, INTEGRITY AND BLACKMAIL

In 1962, when I was a ten-year-old towhead, I attended Mrs. Saiers' fifth-grade class in my little town of Canoe Place. I liked Mrs. Saiers a whole lot, and I thought she liked me, too.

On the second day of school, Lorna Culver and I were chosen to work on the bulletin board out in the hallway. It was a privilege to do so, and only Lorna and I, two out of thirty-one students, were chosen. It's true that when I had volunteered, I sat as still as possible, staring ahead with a stone expression, my arm straight up and motionless. But that's not why Mrs. Saiers chose me. I knew it was because she liked me.

Lorna and I were given free rein over the art closet. Toward the end of each year, the art closet—and art class for that matter—became a little discouraging. Miss Owen, our part-time, roving art instructor, was an innovative teacher. But it had to be difficult at the end of the year to come up with two months of creative ideas of things you could make with empty glue bottles and tacks. But today, the eighth of September, the closet was full of colored construction paper, crayons and even a bottle of glitter (the first I'd ever seen).

Lorna and I decided to make a large "Welcome Back" sign, surrounded by falling leaves, footballs and, in keeping with the autumn theme, a small triceratops in the upper corner (the dinosaur was my idea).

Lorna was up on the ladder, fastening the last falling leaf, when I discovered a tack that had no point. It was just the head, which, lying flat in my palm, created an illusion of severe pain.

"Oh, Lorna," I feigned, "look at my hand. Oh, no! I can't stand it!"

It's remarkable what gravity can do to an unconscious body. Lorna hit the floor like a lump of warm clay, just as Mrs. Saiers came through the door.

"Well, children, how are my artists?" she said with a smile, not yet noticing that one of us was dead. "Oh, my goodness! Lorna! Dear!"

Mrs. Saiers knelt down and rolled Lorna's limp body over. "Bobby, what happened?"

"I-I d-d-don't know," I trembled, tears filling my eyes. "I just showed Lorna my . . ." And opening my hand for Mrs. Saiers to see, I watched at about three-quarter speed as her face turned the color of a dirty chalkboard, and she rolled her eyeballs back in her head, sharing a part of herself with me I'd never known. Lorna was just coming to when Mrs. Saiers sort of slumped down on top of her. This was a brand new experience for Lorna, too, who now lay in the corner beneath her sleeping teacher.

If this had happened the year before in the fourth grade, my teacher, Mrs. Fudd, would have reprimanded me sternly and carried me by the skin on the back of my neck to the principal's office. My principal, Mr. Peligrini, would have looked over my shoulder as I copied a letter to my parents expressing my sincere desire to transfer to a nearby military academy.

But for some reason, Mrs. Saiers liked me. "Oh, you character!" she said with a faint laugh as Sherry Sullivan, who wanted to be a nurse when she grew up, daubed Mrs. Saiers' forehead with a wet paper towel.

What more proof did I need that she liked me?

A few days later, at an all-boys' assembly program, Mr. Peligrini told us fifth-graders he was looking for "a few good young men." He encouraged us to be all that we could be and find our future as patrol boys.

He said, "Ask not what your school can do for you; ask what you can do for your school."

I didn't know why he said that line with a funny accent. But it didn't matter; I was stirred by his speech and felt I had something to strive for.

The patrol boys were an elite group of the very best Arnold Avenue School had to offer. Only twelve boys were chosen from the fifth and sixth grades to be highly trained in pedestrian safety. They carried long, menacing poles with red flags tied to the end, and they wore pure silver, state-issued badges on white patrol sashes across their chests and were given the authority to stop irresponsible students at the crosswalk and report vagrants directly to Mr. Peligrini. They were Mr. P's handpicked squad, and nobody messed with the patrol boys.

It was rumored, though I never believed it, that on being commissioned, each boy was told Mr. Peligrini's first name. I didn't believe any child knew Mr. P's first name. During the twelve years he had been the principal, perhaps as many as 150 boys had gone through the patrol ranks. If that many knew his first name, surely some deviant junior higher would have leaked it by now. But no one had.

At least twice a month, we were given blue mimeographed sheets to take home to our parents. As a distribution ritual, all of us would take the sheets passed over the head of the student in front of us, shove the whole pile to our noses for a whiff, remove the top one for ourselves, and "two-hand" it overhead to the student behind. (We had been doing this for years, and we did it well.) Then we would scan the copy informing our parents of an important meeting of the PTA. At the bottom we would read the signature, L. Peligrini, Principal.

Often when the hall was filled with children and Mr. P was at his post, one of the older boys would look slightly past him and shout down the hall, "Hey, Larry" or "Hey, Leonard." The boy hoped that Mr. Peligrini would look his way and therefore reveal the truth. But he never did.

The patrol-boy selection process would take two weeks. Mr. Peligrini would watch us all carefully, and consulting with our teachers about our academic progress and in-class behavior, he would make his selections. These would be posted on the bulletin board outside the main office.

I had never wanted anything so badly in my life. To think I might be given the privilege of getting up in the dark on winter mornings and walking to school through blizzards that would turn back lesser boys. That I would enter the school early with Mr. Lewis, the custodian, and, together with the "chosen few," select my pole from the closet marked "Mr. P's Patrol." That I would walk proudly eight or nine more blocks to "my corner," where I would serve my principal, my school and my country.

And that wasn't all! After two years of flawless service, I would board a yellow school bus before dawn and ride seven hours to Washington, D.C., where, together with my squad, I would be given a four-hour tour of the White House; the Capitol (both the House and the Senate); the postal department; the Treasury; Arlington Cemetery; the Washington, Jefferson and Lincoln Memorials and eat a free bag lunch before returning home.

My hope was exhilarating, but my fear weakened my knees as I stood with at least fifty others, watching Mr. Peligrini post the tiny list. It read:

1. Capt. Mark Rackish – Arnold Ave. east corner
2. Craig Mundy – Arnold Ave. west corner
3. Barry Burgason – Maple St.
4. Mark Elliot – Broad St.
5. David Kanally – Chestnut
6. Dale Caskey – Keating Ave.
7. Bobby Stromberg – alternate

A small group cheered. Most just walked away. I stood there in disbelief, my eyes full of tears, sobs threatening to burst through my chest. I felt a hand on my shoulder.

"So, Bobby, are you proud you made the squad?"

It was Mrs. Saiers, who obviously didn't understand. Being an alternate wasn't exactly "making the squad." The alternate was only called on if a regular was sick. Everyone knew that due to greater responsibilities and the resultant heightened resistance to viral strains, patrol boys were hardly ever sick.

Only once in my memory had an alternate been promoted to full-time service, and that was when one of the regulars moved away. But the family names on this list had lived in Canoe Place almost since the beginning, and I knew they weren't going anywhere.

But that wasn't what bothered me most. At that moment I didn't care that I wouldn't be able to sacrifice my early morning sleep and after-school playtime, or even that I would miss out on the best trip of my life. It was that the other boys had been deemed worthier than I.

"I just don't get it," I said with a sob. "I just don't understand. Mr. Peligrini said he would watch us closely. What did he see in me that wasn't good enough?"

"Oh, Bobby," she said, kneeling down and wiping my eyes with her doily, "I'm sure it's not that you're not good enough."

"Well then, what is it? Why did he pick these—"

And then the truth hit me so hard I nearly lost my breath. Anger burned through my brush cut, igniting little fire needles on my scalp. Right before my eyes, I saw in the list what Mr. Peligrini had hidden so well with his rousing speech to all of us boys.

He knew all along who would be chosen. I had been deceived. It had nothing to do with our behavior or our work. The squad had been chosen by their street addresses. Right down the list it went.

"Rackish and Mundy, Arnold Ave.," I mumbled. "Kanally, Chestnut. Elliot, Broad. Caskey, Burgason . . ."

They all lived near the corners they had been assigned.

As I looked from beneath my brow, I saw the same truth hit Mrs. Saiers. Her jaw dropped, and she became that chalky color I'd seen only weeks before.

"Excuse me," she said, forcing a smile as she tried to conceal her shock. "You need to run along, and of course, I have some things I need to do." Then almost cheerily, "Congratulations; see you in the morning."

She walked into the office and, without knocking, marched directly through the door marked "L. Peligrini."

As the glass rattled in the slammed door, I heard the muffled, arguing voices of my teacher and principal.

Mrs. Saiers: "mufflemufflemufflemuffleShocked! You told those boys thatmufflemufflemuffle."

Mr. P: "Now, now, I muttermuttermuttermuttermutterGeographic considerationsmuttermutter."

This went on for quite a while as I stood by the bulletin board. I wasn't where I could see into the outer office, but I could hear enough to know I shouldn't be there. Finally the door flew open, and Mr. Peligrini's black, polished shoes, echoing on the hardwood floors, came quickly. There was no time to shoot for the front entrance or even run the six steps to my classroom.

"No, Mrs. Saiers!" he snapped, stopping for emphasis. And then coming again, "We will not discuss this further."

Then he was there, his solid gold belt buckle right in my face. The buckle had a fancy swirl forming the letters "L.P."

It all happened so quickly. I looked up prayerfully into Mr. P's astonished face. Mrs. Saiers rounded the corner, completely unaware of my presence.

Loudly she protested, "But Leslie!"

Mr. Peligrini closed his eyes and sighed with his whole body, the way a criminal might do. He realized he had been caught, and there was no reason to continue the game. It was all over.

Mr. Peligrini's first name was Leslie! There was no doubt in my mind that I was the only child in the history of Arnold Avenue School to know the truth. Not even the patrol boys, under sworn oath and the threat of dishonorable flunking, could have kept this secret. The man's name was Leslie!

I did not understand the concept of blackmail, but I think Mr. Peligrini and Mrs. Saiers did.

Trying hard to conceal her amusement, my favorite teacher said, "Mr. Peligrini, I think it would be so much safer if we had one more patrol boy posted by the bus entrance. Don't you agree?"

Still motionless, staring toward the ceiling, he answered, "Yes, Mrs. Saiers, I think Bobby could begin tomorrow morning."

I became a patrol boy because Mrs. Saiers was willing to become my advocate. Until this event, I'd never realized that adults could be unfair and dishonest, even toward children. I might have become angry and then bitter or distrusting, and, who knows, that might have changed my whole life. But Mrs. Saiers would not allow it to happen.

I liked Mrs. Saiers a whole lot, and I knew she liked me, too.

P.S. Patrol boy wasn't all it was cracked up to be. Neither was our trip to Washington. What I remember most is throwing up on the bus.

P.P.S. I never told his name.

P.P.P.S. Until now!

CHAPTER NINE

THE ANNUAL SCIENCE FAIR

I t's really important, Dad!" Under one arm my son Lars carried a cardboard box containing two houseplants. Under the other arm he carried his poster rolled up in a red rubber band.

"Hurry up, you guys! We have to be on time," he said excitedly, handing the box to his mom and scooting into the back seat. "This counts for half my grade for the whole marking period."

I knew this was important to him. A fourth-grade boy does not dress up in his best clothes, comb his hair without being told and drag the rest of the family, including a less than thrilled older brother, back to school on a Friday night unless it's important.

This was the annual science fair, and I might have been excited myself had my son given me a little more lead time. When I was a kid, the annual science fair was either anticipated or dreaded all year long. But it was never far from our thoughts, and not just because it bore so heavily on our grade.

When I was a child, we understood that doing our best in the science fair had something to do with protecting our national security.

I remember one chilly, moonless, late-autumn night as a five-year-old, lying on top of a thick woolen blanket in my grandparents' gently sloping backyard. We were staring up into a sky so brightly shining that short shadows lay beneath the line of birch.

"What are we looking for, Dad?" I whispered as if my voice might scare it away.

"Whoa!" shouted my sister, sitting up and pointing as two meteors shot long across the sky. "Did you see that? Was that it?!"

"No, no," my dad said quietly. "Lie down, look straight ahead, and we'll see it soon."

Having enjoyed an occasional science fiction comic book in the barber shop, I was starting to feel a little bit concerned.

"Dad," I whispered, snuggling a little closer to my mother's side, "will it look like a real spaceship?"

Before he could answer, my sister was back up on her knees, pointing just above the horizon. "There!" she said in a hard whisper, frozen, pointing just the way she would at a fawn feeding in the backyard. "Right there! Do you see it?"

"That's it," said my dad. "I can't believe it."

"Where?" I shouted.

"Ooooooo, yes, look!" said my mom. Up on her knees with her cheek pressed tightly against my own, she pointed over my shoulder. "Right there! Straight up from the corner pine."

And there it was, a lonely little star, moving across the night sky. No matter how hard we tried we couldn't hear it, so it wasn't an airplane.

Besides, as my sister pointed out, "It's not flashing on and off either."

No, this was something entirely new. This was the first satellite. It belonged to Russia, and my dad said it would change our world forever.

And what do you know, it did. The next year our school joined others across the land as the United States began its game of catch-up with the Russians. Part of the game plan was our very own annual science fair.

We understood as children that we were the future scientists. All of us had stood helplessly and marveled at the tiny point of light moving through the night over our rooftops, vivid proof that we as a nation had fallen behind. It was our task as students at Arnold Avenue School to study science and one day put our country back on top, where God surely intended it to be. It was a burden we proudly bore.

And now, almost thirty-five years later, I drove with my own family to the great event, The Peterson School Annual Science Fair.

"What a way to spend a Friday night," moaned my junior-higher, pouting in the back seat.

Gazing at his two house plants, Lars didn't seem to notice his brother's comment. "Dad," he said, "I hate to tell you this, but I don't think we should have chosen to do this project."

"Well, son," I said, trying hard not to sound defensive, "first of all, *we* didn't choose this project; *you* did. And second, if you had brought home the sheet from your teacher two months ago when the assignment was given to you instead of Tuesday, we could have done any number of things from *my* books."

Late Tuesday evening I had become aware of his oversight after responding to my wife shouting from the boy's bedroom, *"It's due when?!"*

Seconds later I was out of the tub, almost dried but fully dressed. Lars and I were on our way to the library, hoping to find some ideas.

The librarian was not thrilled to see us two minutes before closing but quickly directed us to the section where she quickly said we would quickly be able to find what we needed. Then she added, "Please, quickly."

I was surprised to find my frustration giving way to elation as there before me, in the long row of science books, stood two of the very ones I had used in the fourth grade.

"All right, buddy, now we're cookin'," I said, waving the books at my son.

"Whadja find, Dad?" he asked, continuing to pull others at random and tossing them on the table, under the glaring eye of the librarian.

"Grab one more that looks good to you," I said, "and we're out of here."

Back home at the kitchen table, I displayed the two books to my wife the way I might have some long-lost family heirloom. I could hardly believe it. These were copies of the same ones I had used as a boy.

Oh, to be sure, they weren't in nearly as good a shape as they had been the day I first opened the shiny, stiff covers. I remembered breaking them in by carefully pressing back ten pages at a time.

But they were the same books. Looking at the line drawings of beakers on the front and the stylized typesetting, which was remarkably similar to that on the front of my dad's old '57 Chevy, I felt once again the thrill of learning. The two books were classics called *Hey, Kids, Let's Experiment* and *Science Projects for Fourth Graders of All Ages*.

As I beheld these treasures of my youth, Lars hurriedly leafed through the book he had chosen, hoping to find a project that could be done in two and a half evenings. His book was a 1988 publication entitled *Science Projects That Will Help You to Pass*.

"Here's one, Dad," he said. "I think this will almost work."

I saw no reason to argue with him. My old books, filled with dozens of intricate experiments and complex directions, were no competition for the new book filled with mostly colored pictures.

The experiment he chose was supposed to take a full week, but with a certainty only a desperate boy could possess, he said, "Oh yeah, Dad; no problem. I'm sure we can speed things up a little."

I had never heard the word *stomata* before. Stomata are little holes on a leaf through which a plant breathes in carbon dioxide and breathes out oxygen. The experiment was designed to prove that stomata are located on a leaf's underside. By rubbing Vaseline on the leaves' topside on plant 1 and on the leaves' underside on plant 2, a young scientist can observe within a week's time the slow death of plant 2. This proves that the stomata, on the underside, were plugged up and unable to allow an exchange of gasses.

As I parked near the school gymnasium entrance, Lars expressed his concern for plant 2. "I wish this dumb thing would hurry up and die!"

He fingered the heavy leaves, which he had weighed down with Vaseline about half an inch thick to "speed things up a little."

From behind me, his brother spoke his second full sentence of the evening. "Why don't you just let me step on it?"

We were a little late, but there wasn't much to putting the two healthy plants in the middle of the table and taping the poster up on the wall. Then I looked around and beheld the wonder of the Peterson School Annual Science Fair.

It was impossible, even for my older boy, to avoid getting caught up in the evening's excitement. There were perhaps seventy displays, and to my delight, some were from *my* old books. I saw a boy's papier-mâché volcano, just like my buddy Neil Binder made years ago. I smelled the vinegar and baking soda lava foaming down onto the floor. Of course, real volcanoes hardly ever involve vinegar and baking soda, but it looked as if the boy's mom had done a nice poster to show that he understood the actual process.

I saw miniature oil derricks, utilizing tiny, battery-powered electric engines, pumping black liquid through clear, plastic surgical tubing.

I saw a very nice snake skeleton made from a coat hanger, and right next to it the old faithful homemade electromagnet. I saw a project demonstrating parallel electrical circuitry, the same complex project Danny Manning's dad got him an A + for in 1963. And sure enough, behind the display was a nervous little boy and a proud, smiling dad, answering everyone's questions. It was like going back in time.

If I had just kept my mouth shut and walked away, my nostalgia-induced trance might have convinced me that all was still well with the world. Children still love to learn, and parents and teachers still delight in seeing it happen.

But I had to ask questions. I spotted two jittery little girls talking to some parents by a sign that read "Does the Loch Ness Monster Really Exist?"

I'd always wondered that myself, so I waited for the crowd to move by and then, smiling, I asked them in my most nonthreatening tone, "So, girls, what did you find out? Does he?"

One of the girls shot me a frightened glance, as the other snapped back, "What?"

"I said, 'Does he?'" I explained, "Does he really exist? The monster?"

The girls whispered, asking one another's counsel on how to best answer the question.

"He might," said the bolder of the two. "We don't really know."

"Well," I continued, showing my honest interest, "what did you find out? What can you tell me about the old guy?"

"We proved our hypothesis," said the shy one, looking for her parents.

"And what was that?" I asked.

"That we don't really know," she said. "Maybe he does, maybe he doesn't. We proved that we're not really sure."

Well, it was kind of hard to argue with that, so I walked next door to two rough-looking, roundish boys standing beside a display entitled "The Wonderful World of Friction." The boys were rolling different objects down a ramp they had constructed by leaning a piece of vinyl rain gutter on top of a few cement blocks.

During the time I'd been talking to the girls, the boys had been playing with their experiment, having a ball. Now, as I stood in front of them, they looked as if I'd just turned on the bright lights for the interrogation.

"So, boys, what do we have here?" I chuckled, reading their sign aloud, "The Wonderful World of Friction."

Since I had answered my own question, neither boy felt obligated to.

"What are you doing here, fellas?"

"We were jutht playin'," lisped the chunkier of the two.

"I noticed that," I said. "What were you playing with?"

"Our friction experiment," said the designated spokesman, who spoke very quickly. "We were just rollin' things down the gutter to see about friction, and we found out that smooth things like steelies and marbles roll faster than sticky things like this ball of Play-Doh or clay or mashed potatoes or some—"

"Yeah," the other interrupted, "and that proovth it."

"It proves what?" I asked.

"That it workth," he said, the sweat beading on his forehead.

"What works?" I pressed.

"The friction," said the spokesman, almost cowering. "It proves it."

And so my conversations went most of the evening. To be fair, some students actually understood the premise of their projects and were able to state their hypothesis and articulate their findings. A few even seemed to be having fun. But mostly an oppression sapped all the life right out of the evening.

At first I thought it must be me. *I must be intimidating these poor kids in some way*, I thought.

But no, even when I approached a table with nothing but smiles and praise, I watched the color wash right out of the child's face. It transported me to the only time I recall from my boyhood that offered any explanation.

On a hot August evening, on the baseball diamond back in my hometown, I was eleven years old, playing right field. I was the worst player on a pretty good team.

All summer I'd been lucky enough to have very few balls hit my way. That's why I was chosen to play out there. Very few balls are hit into right field in Little League.

To my relief, in the last inning of our most important game, once again nothing crucial had flown in my direction. Furthermore, I was home free because I probably wouldn't have to bat again.

"Fine with me!"

Unfortunately, ten minutes later I was walking to the plate with an opportunity to keep us in the game or end our season.

"It's up to you, Bobby," said my coach, knowing there was no way.

I hadn't really hit the ball all year long. Several times I'd closed my eyes and swung about the time the ball was nearing the plate. Miraculously, the ball intersected the arc of my swing at the proper point, making contact with the bat at the thinnest part. The electrical shock of pain from the violently vibrating wood shot open my eyes in time to see the pitcher picking up the ball at his feet and tossing it in a long, slow lob over to first base. Those were my good games.

Now, as I walked toward the plate, I heard the encouraging mumbles of my teammates discussing their hopes for my success. "Oh, well, Harvey, you wanna go to the Tastee Freeze?"

Several of our team parents were packing their younger kids into the station wagons. The fans of our opponents shouted joyfully to their pitcher, "Okay, Bucky! Easy out! Easy out!"

While I stood at the plate, their coach stopped the game momentarily to yell to his outfield, "Move it in, guys! No, no, *way in*! Come on! Move in!"

The pitcher, a tall, lanky kid with a mustache, hurled the ball at blinding speed right at my head. At the last moment I arched my back, throwing my body into the dust, certain I'd been hit, certain I'd be trotting triumphantly to first base.

The umpire watched the ball curve straight down the middle and shouted, "STEEEEEE-RIIIIIIIKE!!!" The fans went crazy.

The last two pitches were slow balls. At least I think they were. They seemed to take about five minutes to get from the mound to the plate. I could see the stitching on the slowly rotating ball. I could hear my coach screaming, "Take a cut, Bobby. Now!"

I wanted to swing, but I didn't. I wanted to risk it all, stand there with a smile on my lips, point to the outfield and say, "See that spot, Bucky? It's goin' right there."

But I didn't. I stood there, a pasty color, afraid to take a swing as the ball floated by.

My reasoning was "If I swing the bat, I might miss the ball."

Now, at the annual science fair, I saw two jittery little girls by their Loch Ness display; two abrasive little round guys who seemed to understand little about friction; and a shy boy who might have been able to tell me a whole lot about parallel circuitry if his dad would have just stopped talking.

Now I understood. The kids didn't want to go to the plate and take their stance in front of the teachers, their parents or me. None of them dared to risk it all and say, "Let me tell you what I learned, 'cause I learned a bunch."

Instead they struck out without taking a cut at the ball. Their reasoning was "If I try to tell them what I know, I might be wrong."

The fear of failure stole all the joy of learning.

I returned home that evening with mixed feelings. On the one hand, I was depressed, and I felt bad for those children who had worked so hard and enjoyed it so little.

On the other, I felt pretty good about Lars. He actually understood how plants breathed and was anxious to tell the little bit he knew to anybody he could find. I'm glad he's that kind of child.

Several days later he was thrilled to show me a dead plant 2. I'm not sure if it had suffocated the way it was supposed to or if the two pounds of Vaseline had broken its will to live.

I won't forget the evening. It encouraged me, a middle-aged, comfortable guy, to take a few risks. It encouraged me to be a father who helps his children keep the world in perspective. It made me grateful to realize it doesn't matter whether I go down swinging or freeze at the plate; God doesn't throw me off the team. All in all, I think I learned more at my son's fair than I did at my own.

CHAPTER TEN

MARLA FARBER: A FIGURE OF SPEECH

Marla Farber was fifteen years old and obese. She was, as they say, nearly as wide as she was tall, and possessed no redeeming pretty face, personality or intellect. It's hard to imagine she had a friend, for nothing about her was attractive.

Besides her weight problem, she was not clean. Her hair lay matted flat like wet fur on a long-haired cat. She wore the same clothes everyday, and no one questioned if she might have several identical outfits. (Students within a couple of seats of her in homeroom knew for certain she did not.)

Her complexion was the kind doctors took slides of for medical conventions. With her crooked teeth she continually chewed her fingernails, painfully gnawing them back until there was nothing left, and still she did not stop.

Her remarkably thick, black-rimmed glasses would not stay put on her slippery nose, and every five seconds she'd take a nubby finger out of her mouth to shove them back up.

I never met Marla Farber. I never even saw her, which seems odd to me since Judy and I have used her name often. We still do.

Sometimes we use her name as a noun. "I met a girl this weekend who was kind of a Marla Farber."

More often, though, we use it as an adjective. "It was one of those painful Marla Farber situations."

Always we use her name gently.

Marla and Judy were in Miss Colodney's tenth-grade homeroom, but that was about all they had in common. When Judy walked to school on the first day of class, surrounded by her good friends, she was tall, pretty and smiling, for it was a happy time in her life.

Earlier in the spring, her parents had taken her aside and shared with her the wonderful news that she was again going to become a big sister. She'd been through this three times before, but this time was special. The last time a child was born in her family, Judy had been eight years old and unable to fully appreciate what was happening. But at fifteen she could almost imagine having a baby herself and delightedly marveled as her mom grew large over the summer months.

Now, on the first day of school, she sat in the stuffy third-floor homeroom and waited for the bell to ring. To her right, a fat girl chewed on her fingers. To her left, her best friend, Kathy, studied her morning schedule and asked, "So how's your mom doing?"

"She's doing great!" Judy said. "Did you see her in church? She's really getting big."

"I know," Kathy said with a giggle. "I couldn't believe it! When's she due?"

"Not until the end of October!"

"October! Oh, she's going to be enormous!"

The bell rang, and Miss Colodney said, "Good morning, students." Quickly Kathy whispered, "Promise me I can be your first friend to see the baby."

Pulling her long legs under the desk, Judy mouthed, "I promise," though they both knew it was unnecessary.

Across the aisle Marla shoved her glasses back up on her nose.

Each morning more classmates asked about the expected child, and as the end of October approached, their questions became shorter.

"Anything?"

"No baby?"

"Good news?"

Finally one morning, accompanied by girlish squeals and happy hugs, the questions became more specific.

"Boy or girl?"

"What's his name?"

"Oh, is he cute?"

Judy answered, "His name is Paul Andrew, and he's so precious."

Then a thick, mannish voice no one had heard before asked, "When can we come see him?"

Everyone turned to see Marla looking straight at Judy. Though she looked no better on this morning than any other, she did seem oddly unlike herself. Never before had she lifted her gaze beyond her desk top or stared intently beyond her nubby fingers. But now her eyes were steady, and she waited for an answer.

Even if Judy had been able to find one, she could not have spoken it, for her breath was gone. Marla Farber had asked, "When can *we* come see him?" That thought was like an unexpected hard right to the rib cage.

A few students turned toward Judy, wondering how she would respond. Others, embarrassed, glanced away and leafed through homework. Still Marla waited for an answer.

"Well, I promised that Kathy could come first, and . . . and . . . my mom is having to take it easy for a week or so . . . but . . . after that . . . I'm sure that anyone who . . . who . . . anyone . . ."

She was against the ropes. Every second Marla waited was another blow, and Judy was stumbling, about to give in, about to say, "Okay! You win! You can come today." Then the bell rang, giving her a moment in her own corner, a chance to breathe deeply and gain some composure.

Miss Colodney took attendance. They all stood and mumbled the pledge. After class Judy left, hoping Marla would think the conversation had just been sidetracked. No malice intended. The question had merely been forgotten.

But it was not to be.

Each morning Marla continued her assault with new questions.

"Could I come home with you for lunch?"

"Would Friday be a good day?"

"Do you have some free time after school?"

"How about this evening?"

As the weeks passed, Judy knew all her excuses were sounding as lame as they really were, especially since each new morning several more girls and even a few of the boys talked about how cute the baby was.

Day after day Marla persisted, "I'm not doing anything on Saturday. How about Saturday? Or today. Today would actually be good!"

Judy held her off one week by creating a bad flu bug from a baby's sniffle, and another week by creating a migraine for her mom from a slight headache. But Marla was willing to wait.

"Is little Pauly over the flu?"

"Is your mom better now?"

First there was guilt. *Why don't I just invite her over?* Judy thought. *Is she any less valuable than anyone else? I know I should* reach out to her. If ever anyone needed love and friendship, it's Marla.

Eventually, however, the guilt gave way to anger. *How dare she call him "Pauly," as if she's one of the family! Is she so stupid she can't see I don't want her in my house? Do I have to come out and tell her I don't want her grubby hands anywhere near my baby brother? Do I have to come out and actually say it?*

The answer was yes. She probably did have to actually say it, and that was something she could not do.

"Honey, what's the matter?" her mom asked as Judy burst through the door after school in tears.

The whole story spilled out in sobs over the kitchen table. "Oh, Mom, I feel so awful, and I know I shouldn't treat her this way, but she's so filthy, and she won't stop, and I just couldn't stand to think of her anywhere near the baby. Oh, I'm so sorry."

Pulling a chair close and putting her arm around her daughter, her mom said gently, "Well, it sounds to me as though she's not going to let this go away. So why don't you invite her over on Friday, and she can come in for a minute. Then this will be over."

So Friday afternoon the tall, pretty girl and the fat, ugly one walked home from school together. Knowing the ordeal would be over soon made it no easier for Judy, but at least her mom had said she could come in "for a minute." It only had to be a minute. They would walk through the kitchen and into the nursery. Marla could take a quick look at the baby and leave. It would only take a minute.

Marla, working hard and wheezing to keep up, asked questions nonstop. "So how's your mom? Is Pauly sleeping better? Do you get to baby-sit?"

Judy answered as quickly as she could. None of it was Marla's business.

She can come in for a minute, Judy thought. *It will only take a minute.*

They climbed the back porch steps and opened the kitchen door.

"Oh, there you are!" her mom greeted them cheerily.

As Marla entered behind Judy, Judy began to roll her eyes back for her mother's benefit, when surprised, she noticed her mom was wearing her newest dress.

"And this must be Marla," she said with open arms. "I'm so glad you could come home with Judy. Sit down, girls, and have some fresh cookies."

"Fresh cookies? Mom, you made fresh cookies?" Judy was incredulous, feeling her emotions close to the edge. Her mom had said it would only take a minute. Marla only had to stay a minute. So why had Mom made fresh cookies?

"Paul's still sleeping," her mom said, pulling a chair out first for Marla and then for Judy. "So why don't you sit down, girls, and this will give us a chance to get acquainted a little bit. He should wake up in just a minute."

But he didn't wake up in just a minute. He didn't even wake up in twenty minutes, as Marla ate a dozen cookies and asked stupid questions one on top of the other. "Does he take a nap everyday? Does he eat real food? Does he crawl? Can he talk? Will he wake up pretty soon?"

Judy's mom smiled and patiently answered question after question as if Marla were her best friend.

Judy caught her mom's eye and gave a pained expression as if to say, "Please, Mom! It was only going to take a minute! Remember?"

"Well," her mom said, taking the hint, "I guess he's not going to wake up after all, so come on in Marla, and we'll introduce you two."

The nursery was bright and clean and smelled of baby powder as Judy stood in the doorway and watched Marla and her mom peer into the tiny crib.

Okay, she thought, *that's good. She's seen him. No reason to wake him up. Let's go!*

But her mom reached into the crib and gently pulled back the soft blanket. The baby lay sleeping face down with his skinny legs tucked up beneath him and his diapered bottom sticking up in the air.

Marla, smiling, gasped a single "Oh!" and then stood silently, her glasses about to fall off her nose.

Judy started to whisper, "Let's not wake—," but her mom had already started to ask Marla the question.

"Would you like to hold him?"

It was almost more than Judy could take. *Would you like to hold him?!* she thought. *This whole thing only had to take a minute. You just walk in, and you walk out. But no, Mom had to dress up and make cookies and answer questions, and now, of all things, she has to ask if Marla would like to hold him.*

Judy couldn't figure out how her mom could be so insensitive. How could she let Marla touch her own baby? What was she thinking?

"Marla," her mom asked again, "would you like to hold him?"

Marla didn't answer. She didn't even acknowledge she'd heard. Judy's mom reached down, rolled the baby over, lifted him gently and laid him in Marla's fat arms.

Frozen in wide-eyed wonder like a child holding a fragile soap bubble, her face only inches from the miracle, Marla gazed on the sleeping baby boy and whispered over and over, "Oh! Oh! Oh!"

Moments later, with a smile on her face, she gingerly returned the baby, left the room, took another cookie, said, "Thank you" and walked down the back stairs.

She didn't ask, "Can I come back?"

She didn't say, "I'll talk to you tomorrow, Judy."

She just left. The pretty girl and the ugly girl shared few words ever again.

But Marla was not forgotten. Judy and I still speak of her often. In fact, hardly a month goes by that we don't say her name.

Sometimes we use it as a noun. "I met a girl this weekend who is kind of a Marla Farber."

More often we use it as an adjective. "It was one of those painful Marla Farber situations."

Always we use her name gently. For Marla Farber has become for us a figure of speech, a reminder of the sacrificial love Jesus calls us all to give.

CHAPTER ELEVEN

STARTING SOMEWHERE

S ometimes the old creative juices dry right out, and I begin to wonder if I'll ever write another song or find another funny bit or create another story. That's when it's helpful to look back.

It's true, you know. It's true you've got to start somewhere. And chances are pretty good your first attempts at anything will not produce greatness. But you plug away, and one day you look back, and by golly, you've improved. That's kind of encouraging.

I've been writing songs for nearly twenty-five years now, and though no one other than myself has shown much interest in recording them or even singing them, for cryin' out loud, I'm kind of encouraged these days.

I started early. Like so many boys in the fifties searching for an identity, I found my role model in the world of music. There he was, smilin' out through the Motorola, playing effortlessly, his instrument an extension of his very self. The crowd was spinning, dancing, connecting with his unique sound. He was "The King." As I watched him faithfully with my grandparents, I knew that one day I, too, would play the accordion like Myron Floren.

And I did. I played it for seven years. I might have played it the rest of my life, but when I was twelve, I went away to summer camp. I was becoming interested in girls, and there were some there.

You know the setting . . . the last night of camp, around the fire down on the beach, boats shiftin' key downwind, breeze blowin' in off the lake, a few boys and girls actually sitting close together, and handsome college counselors playing guitars as we sang songs. Folk songs. Romantic folk songs. (At least they seemed romantic, though it may have been hormones.) We sang as if unaware of our limited adolescent vocal capabilities.

> Michael row the boat ashore
> Alleluia

We sang.

> Michael row the boat ashore
> Alleluia

We swayed together.

> Sister help to trim the sail
> Alleluia

We stared into the dying embers, transfixed. Zombies.

> River Jordan is chilly and cold
> Alleluia
Chills the body but not the soul
> Alle luuuuu uuuuuuuuuuuuuuuuu yaaaaaaaaaaaaaaaaaaaah

Our voices trailed off as if consumed by the fire. It was a sacred moment, and in the awesome silence, we were one.

Then I stood up with my accordian and played "Beer Barrel Polka" and "Lady of Spain."

I left camp the following morning realizing I had no friends under seventy and prepared to tell my parents I could no longer play the accordion. I wanted to play the guitar, and I bought one with my own money.

It cost me $14.50 brand new. Interestingly enough, even in the early sixties, this was not a quality instrument. But it was on this instrument that I wrote my very first song.

By the way, I no longer have that guitar. Actually, I do have it, but I don't play it often. You see, the following Christmas (my thirteenth), I was realizing the importance of developing a macho image. It was time for me to learn how to hunt.

Unfortunately, my father didn't hunt. And my mother didn't hunt. And my older sister didn't hunt with a gun. But my parents came up with a compromise. Instead of a gun under the Christmas tree, I received a bow.

The following year I received an arrow. I noticed on the box that the bow was thirty-pound test. It wasn't a big bow, and frankly I wondered if thirty pounds would be powerful enough to damage the charging bear and moose I planned to stalk in camouflaged masculinity.

I didn't dare test it outside, because there was snow, and I knew if I lost the arrow I'd probably have to wait another year to get a new one.

Fortunately, on my dresser, under my junior-high letter sweater, I found a large pumpkin left over from Halloween. It didn't look like a pumpkin. It was all flat, green and fuzzy. I wondered if thirty-pound test would be powerful enough to penetrate what had once been, after all, a living creature.

Having removed the rubber suction cup my father said was "simply for your own protection," I placed the arrow on the string.

Taking aim, I pulled back steadily. Twenty-nine pounds . . . thirty pounds . . . thirty-one . . . maybe thirty-two . . . I let it go.

When the spray settled, all that remained was an eerie sound and a moldy fragrance. The arrow, the fuzz, the seeds, the shell and one pair of socks had disappeared from the top of my dresser. Vanished! Completely gone!

I searched my tiny room for a long time. Had the arrow entered another dimension? And if so, would my parents understand?

Several days later I attempted to remove my guitar from its strap where it hung on the wall. It wouldn't move. On closer examination, I discovered the arrow had entered my guitar through the sound hole and almost exited completely through the wall paneling behind. The feathers were clearly visible just behind the strings. The pumpkin had been deposited in the bottom of the guitar. The socks remain a mystery to this day.

So I no longer have the guitar. Actually, I do have it, but I don't play it often. It works; it's just really uncomfortable with that arrow poking my chest.

So, anyway, I was thirteen years old. I stood before my parents, my guitar slung low on my hip. My hair hung partially over one eye.

"Mom and Dad," I announced boldly, "I've decided I want to be a professional songwriter."

My parents sat down in unison on the divan.

"And now I would like to perform for you the very first song that I ever just wrote."

I knew two chords. I utilized them both. You might say I gave it everything I had. My melody followed my chord structure note for note.

Oh, you say you're gonna go and see surfer Sam
Oh, you know they say that he's a real neat man
He plays the guitar and he hits the beat
Man, that guy is really neat

My dad was moved. I could tell, because he had his face in his hands, and he was shaking all over.

It's true, you know. It's true you've got to start somewhere. I'm a little further along now than when I began, and that's kind of encouraging.

CHAPTER TWELVE

THE SCREAMIN' LUCY

W e called ourselves "The Lums." I don't recall for certain who came up with the name (probably my buddy Mark). I only know it didn't mean anything, it felt good in the mouth, and we knew it was perfect from the start.

Mark and David and I were the three original Lums, and we did everything together. In the summertime we played on the same Little League baseball team. Though I was not a very good baseball player (largely due to being scared to death of the ball), it really didn't matter, because I was a Lum.

On hot afternoons we used to swim together. Though David was not a very good swimmer (Mark and I both had our "shark badges," so we could go in the deep end, but David only had his "turtle" and had to stay behind the first ropes), it really didn't matter, because he was a Lum.

On warm evenings at about twilight, we used to play Kick the Can. Those who have played the game know that the slowest runner is always "it." So Mark was "it" every night. All night long, all summer long, from May to September, Mark was "it."

But you know what? It really didn't matter, because after all, he was a Lum.

In the winter things slowed down a bit for The Lums, but we walked to school together. And we ate lunch together. And everyday after school, without exception, we would go to L.I.H. (Lums International Headquarters). Actually, it was Mark's garage. There we spent our after-school hours, playing Ping Pong and other more creative, less marketable games of our own devising, like Toss the Frisbee Through the Screen Door or Snap the Mousetrap on Your Snow Boot.

One day Mark brought in the new spring and summer edition of the Sears and Roebuck Catalog. As we leafed through pages filled with pictures of children playing with wonderful, colorful toys, we wondered what it must be like to be one of those kids and to have all those things for our own.

Then we turned a page and saw it. It had high, silver handlebars; a long, white, vinyl banana seat; a large, black, knobby, back tire and green sparkle finish. It was called "The Screamin' Lucy." None of us had ever seen such a bike.

Standing on the pedals in a racing position, staring right out of the picture, was a laughing, happy boy about our age, who looked as if he could have been one of us except he was really clean. Coming out of his mouth past his gleaming teeth was a big cartoon bubble with the words, "Hey, guys! Imagine having one of these!" Well, he didn't have to suggest that, because we already had imagined it, and we liked the idea.

It was the most beautiful bike we had ever seen, and it was expensive! In fact, only one bike in the whole catalog cost more, but it wasn't nearly as flashy.

Instead of the high, silver handle bars, this other bike had little, curly ones that went the wrong way. Instead of the long, white, vinyl banana seat, this other bike had a little, black sliver of a thing that looked as though it would be pretty uncomfortable to sit on for a long period of time. Instead of the fat, black, knobby back tire, this other bike had a little, skinny tube that looked as if it would be pretty hard to balance on. And instead of green sparkles, this other bike was just blue. It was called "The Blue Flyer," and though it was much more expensive, we all agreed it was not nearly as flashy.

I'm quite certain it was Mark's idea. Mark always came up with the big ideas.

He said, "Hey, you guys! What do you say we ask our moms and dads if all three of us can get Screamin' Lucys for our birthdays?"

We had birthdays three days in a row—June 1, June 2 and June 3. According to Mark, who was pretty good in arithmetic, the odds of this happening were six quadzillion to one, which sounded just about right to me.

Well, from that moment on, Mark and David talked of nothing else, and though I tried to share their excitement, I was hardly elated. I knew there was little chance of my getting a Screamin' Lucy. I'd never received a gift that expensive in my life, and I knew that this year my mom and dad were needing to be particularly careful about spending money.

In fact, I never said a thing to my parents about The Lums' big plan until about three weeks before my birthday. I wouldn't even have mentioned it then had my dad not asked me one night at supper, "Well, son, you've got a birthday coming up pretty soon, don't you?"

"Sure do, Dad," I said, hoping the next question would follow.

"Well, what would you like to get for a present this year?"

Only then did I dare say, "Dad, you know Mark and David? Well, Mark and David, the other Lums, well, they're probably going to get

Screamin' Lucy bicycles, you know? And if I really had my wish, I would want to get a new bike, too."

I was expecting to get the standard little speech about finances and house payments and hard times, but instead, to my surprise, my father leaned over, looked me right in my eyes and said, "Well, son . . . we'll see."

In David's family, "we'll see" meant his dad hadn't heard a word David said. In Mark's family, "we'll see" meant "ain't no possible way." But in my family, "we'll see" meant there was still hope, and I was excited!

I could hardly wait for June 1 to arrive. The first birthday was Mark's. We went to his house for supper. I remember we had some hot dogs, Kraft macaroni and cheese, and cake.

Then we all tumbled into the living room, where a large assortment of gifts awaited our friend. He got a lot of little gifts. Of course it was Mark's desire to go toward the larger packages first. This was an inclination shared by us all, but his mom pointed out that "some of the best gifts come in the smallest packages."

I had heard this before, and I supposed she was telling the truth, though I couldn't imagine anything I would want that could fit into boxes so small.

He did get a nice clip-on bow tie and also a pair of pheasant cuff links. But really those things didn't matter too much, because what he had his eye on the whole time was the big box over in the corner.

When all the other gifts were opened, Mark's mother said, "Oh, my goodness, I thought we were all done, but now I see there is still one more. Do you suppose that could be for you, Mark?"

Mark walked over, grabbed that big box, slid it into the middle of the room and tore open the back end. The first thing he saw was a big, black, knobby back tire. And then the long, white, vinyl banana seat; the high handlebars; and the green sparkle finish. He'd gotten the Screamin' Lucy!

But he didn't ride it, because we had made a deal that none of us would ride it until all three had one. One down; two to go.

The next birthday was David's. We went to his house for lunch, where, as I recall, we had some hot dogs, Kraft macaroni and cheese, and a piece of yellow cake. Then we tumbled into the family room, where a large pile of small packages awaited our anxious buddy.

I felt David made out a little better than Mark; he got a nice marine band harmonica. But several of his gifts were awfully predictable, most notably the one he received from his grandma.

We all knew what it was before he opened it by the size of the box and because all of us had many times received the same gift from our grandmas. It was a long, thin box containing three white hand-kerchiefs, with initials in needlepoint stitched on the top corner. Of course they weren't David's initials, but that really wasn't all that important to him, because what he had his eye on the whole time was the big box over in the corner.

"Okay, buddy," announced his dad, "it's the moment we've all been waiting for."

David grabbed that big box, slid it out into the middle of the room and tore open the back end. The first thing he saw was a big, black, knobby back tire. And then the long, white, vinyl banana seat; the high handlebars; and the green sparkle finish. He'd gotten the Screamin' Lucy!

But he didn't ride it, because we had made a deal that none of us would ride it until all three had one. Two down; one to go.

On the third of June, I was a nervous wreck. For about two and a half weeks, I had been looking everywhere in my house. I had looked through the entire basement. I had climbed up into the attic, where my parents kept all the junk they said we might need someday. I had looked in my parents' closet behind my dad's suits and my mom's dresses that hung all the way to the floor. No big box!

We met at my house for breakfast. I don't remember what we ate, but I do remember opening up my last little gift from a great aunt who never understood me very well. It was a book on dating. As I felt the lump growing in my throat, I turned my head toward the sound of my father's footsteps coming down the stairs, and I saw the box! What a thrill! To me it looked bigger than ever!

"Well, son," said my father with an excitement nearly equaling my own, "go ahead. Open it up!"

I grabbed that box, slid it out into the middle of the room and tore open the back end. The first thing I saw was a skinny little tube that looked as if it would be pretty hard to balance on, and then a little, black sliver of a seat that looked as though it would be difficult to sit on for a long period of time, and small handle bars that curled the wrong way, and instead of green sparkles I saw just blue.

As my mom and dad smiled and waited for my response, the reality settled on me like a thunderstorm on a Sunday picnic. I had gotten The Blue Flyer.

I did my best to hide my feelings from my parents, and I must say that the other Lums played right along as only close friends would do.

"Wow!" said Mark, trying hard to act envious. "I mean, boy, oh boy, what I wouldn't give for a bike like that!"

"Yes sireee," said David, as if he were reading off a cue card, "look at them handlebars. We're talkin' curly!"

But my father must have seen through our acting, because he said, "Son, if you would like to trade this bike in for another one, well, I suppose we could do that."

I wanted to say yes! so badly. I wanted to throw my arms in the air and shout, "Yes! Yes! Yes!" But I couldn't, not after I knew my parents had spent so much for me. They had bought me the most expensive bike in the whole Sears and Roebuck Catalog.

"No, Dad," I said, forcing my face to cooperate. "I really, really like The Blue Flyer. I just really like it. What can I say? I mean, it's just really . . . blue."

Well, things were never quite the same again. I was still a Lum. Once you're a Lum you're always a Lum. You just can't get out of something like that. But the other Lums were zippin' around pullin' wheelies on their little Screamin' Lucys, while I could hardly reach the pedals on my big Blue Flyer.

But then, about a month after our birthdays, the chain guards on the Screamin' Lucys started rattling pretty badly. Of course, they were easily repaired, but by the end of the summer, they were rattling again. By the beginning of the following summer, both chain guards fell right off.

David kept getting grease on his ankle, and Mark kept getting his shoelaces caught in the gears. And wouldn't you know it, the green sparkles washed off after the third or fourth good rainfall. Then the situation started getting disturbingly painful when the white vinyl peeled off those metal banana seats. (Mark and David used to park their bikes at the swimming pool, where the hot sun would shine down on those seats, heating the metal to a temperature adequate to prepare a rump roast of any origin.) The handlebars kept slipping way down so the plastic streamers they had put in the handle grips dragged on the ground. By the end of the second summer, both boys took their Screamin' Lucys to the dump, where, with a mighty, spinning heave, they tossed their summer dreams into a pile of scrap metal disappointments.

But my Blue Flyer was as good as new! In fact, it still is. Thirty years later, as my father coasts down the hill in front of his house, the Blue Flyer still makes that clean sound: "Ticka ticka ticka

ticka ticka ticka ticka ticka."

I've often used this story for children's sermons to illustrate how God's best gift to us was not a flashy one. The people were looking for a flashy king with a high, silver crown and long, flowing, green sparkle robes. Instead they received the baby Jesus lying in a manger and the Messiah riding on a donkey. Hardly the flash they had in mind.

To me the analogy seemed fairly obvious. I even tried to carry it further by describing how, as an adult, I returned to my parents' home and discovered my thirty-year-old Blue Flyer hanging on the basement ceiling, still in fine condition. Surely even a small child could understand that just as my bike was not flashy but long lasting, so also Jesus is not flashy but eternal.

Unfortunately, children identified with the story so powerfully they were unwilling to accept any comparison.

Often I would say, "Children, long ago the people were looking for a flashy king, but instead they got Jesus."

(The children would still be with me here; they'd heard this story before.)

"And children," I would continue, "do you remember what Jesus was riding when He entered the city?"

There was never any confusion or hesitation here. Children are not dumb; they knew the answer. Almost in unison they would respond, "The Blue Flyer!"

That usually provided a nice chuckle for all the delighted moms and dads who watched their darling cherubs from the pews. I would then attempt to skillfully get us back on track, adding, "You know, children, just a few weeks ago I was in my parents' home, and do you know what I found hanging on the ceiling in the basement?"

This was a harder question, and I knew it would take a second for the children to think it through. But someone always found the answer. "Oh! Oh! I got it," a rosy-cheeked theologian would yell, waving a frantic arm.

"Yes!" I would say encouragingly. "Do you know what I found hanging there?"

"Yep, I sure do. You found a donkey!"

Well, listen, you can make fun of my bald spot or criticize my driving, but one thing is for sure: This guy knows how to teach!

CHAPTER THIRTEEN

I WAS THERE

I am one of a lucky generation of dads who actually had the opportunity to take part in their children's births. Of course, I realize all fathers through all ages have had some small part in their kids' births. Indeed, if they had not carefully planned ahead and dutifully fulfilled their small part of the bargain, no births would have happened. But I do not write here about this providentially joyous, primary, paternal responsibility. I'm talking about being there at the actual birth.

Many men today take this for granted, as though fathers have always been able to do so. But dads in previous generations were not always so fortunate.

For example, even though my parents were both born upstairs in their family homes, my grandfathers were not permitted to be present in the room. Both my grandmothers were allowed to stay, but their husbands were instructed by the attending doctor to "go boil water."

I'd often heard this command uttered by disheveled old docs in television westerns like "Gunsmoke" or "Bonanza." And even as a child (understanding the little I did about sanitation), I figured the boiling water was to sterilize surgical instruments.

But I've since learned that routine births don't require metal tools. In fact, I should think a hammer, tin snips and lug wrench (whether sterilized or not) would be the last articles a doctor would wish to have within reach of a woman in transition.

No, I think this whole boiling thing was just more medical profession deception. I suspect more was said than "Go boil water."

I think the actual conversation went something like this:

Grandpa (speaking at a frantic speed, sweating through his clothing): Oh, Doc, she's a hurtin'! Oh, gee! Oh, golly! Doc, is it supposed to happen like this? Is it, huh? Is it, huh? Is it? Is it? Is it? Is it?

Grandma (wondering which child is the greater source of pain): Albin, will you shut up? Will you just *shut up*?

Doctor: Albin, I need some cake. Go now! Bake a cake. It's important!

Grandpa (weeping, with his face to the wall): Oh, no, Doc! Oh, now what am I gonna do? I don't know how to bake a cake!

Doctor: Then fry me an egg. Over easy. Quick! Go!

Grandpa (throwing himself face down on Grandma's bed): Oh, Doc! I don't know how to bake an egg either!

Doctor: *Then boil some water! Just leave!*

Grandpa (with confidence, ready to face the challenge): I can do that, Doc! You won't be disappointed.

While my grandfather read carefully through the manual for the new gas range, trying to figure out how to make a flame, my mother was born.

Things actually became worse by the time my parents were waiting for my sisters and me. We weren't even allowed to be born at home. No, my dad had to drive my mom on bald tires twenty-five miles over icy, poorly maintained, mountainous roads in the middle of the night to a hospital so we could be born safely, and even then he wasn't allowed in the same room with my mom, because the doctors didn't want him there.

But they'd created a problem for themselves, because their old line didn't work anymore. They couldn't tell him to drive all the way home through a raging blizzard to boil water. So they created a special place for him down the hallway, where with other nervous, expectant men he could pace back and forth and learn how to smoke cigarettes. It was, for my dad's generation, the proper thing to do.

In fact, if you were actually present at your child's birth, it was probably because you messed up. If you didn't plan well—for example, if you ran out of gas—then you had no choice. You had to be there. This was shameful, because the wonder of experiencing a new life is somewhat diminished when it's happening in the front seat of your new Plymouth or on the church steps or in an airplane or at the state basketball championships. Much better to do your job well, get your wife to the hospital in time, leave her with the doctor and go down to your special little room and try smoking.

But I was there when my children were born.

My wife, Judy, and I had enrolled in a Lamaze natural childbirth class (not to be confused with the LeMans method, which is a noisier, much more rapid approach to giving birth). Once a week during most of our last trimester of pregnancy, we drove to the hospital. There, along with a dozen other men and their swollen, increasingly uncomfortable wives, we prepared for the big day.

I really enjoyed the class. In my sixteen years of formal education, I had never been in a classroom of more motivated students. Our teacher did not need to be inspiring or clever; she already had our complete and undivided attention. Like a class of new paratroopers learning how to properly pack their own chutes, we, too, wanted very much to get it right the first time.

I was particularly pleased that the class was not a lot of theory but experiential, hands-on education. For example, to simulate labor contractions for my wife, I was instructed to grab one of Judy's calf muscles and squeeze hard. Judy then could practice her controlled breathing-relaxation techniques under the pressure of my two-handed grip. It wasn't exactly like the real thing, and the payoff certainly wasn't as great. But the reward for Judy's hard work was a growing confidence that she could be in control and perhaps even enjoy the process of giving birth to our baby.

At the end of each class, our teacher, Ms. Anzaloto, had a special question and answer time for the dads. She asked each of us questions, and we gave the answers in front of the whole class.

I felt that, compared to the other men, I held my own. After all, we're not talking about easy, true-false or obvious, multiple choice questions.

"Robert," she said one evening as I stood before the class, "imagine, if you will, the following scenario. You and Judith have been in the labor room for eighteen hours, the last twelve of which she has suffered hard back labor. You yourself are exhausted, having not slept in more than thirty-two hours. Now you notice that Judith is starting to lose her composure. She has forgotten all about her focal point. Indeed, she is beginning to close her eyes."

"Bad girl!" I said with a smile down at Judy. The rest of the class was amused (these people were easily entertained).

"That's right, Robert," said Ms. Anzaloto. "But now things are getting more serious. Judith is no longer following your coaching. She's given up on her controlled breathing altogether, and her moans are becoming screams. Furthermore, her screaming is being directed at you. She is blaming you for the whole thing, saying she wished she'd never met you. Now, Robert, as her coach, what would you do?"

Several of the other men, with an obvious need to please, shot their hands into the air with an "Ooooo, Oooooo, I know! I know!" And of course they did.

Everyone knew our teacher wanted me to say I would calmly and lovingly talk my wife out of her hysteria. I would firmly encourage her to focus on her focal point and resume her rhythmic breathing. And most importantly, at no time would I speak in condescending tones.

But Ms. Anzaloto had not asked me what I *should* do. She had asked me what I *would* do.

"Well," I answered, "to be very honest, it would be difficult for me to face Judy's screams, particularly those referring directly to me, especially after being up for thirty-two hours. But I recognize that this is not the time to fall apart. This is certainly not the time to scream back. No, this is the time Judy needs me more than ever to help her regain control and get on with the blessed task of bringing a new life into the world."

"Yes, yes, Robert, we know that," pushed my teacher. "Now what would you do?"

"Well, I would immediately employ the very techniques I've practiced so hard in this class," I said, bringing a smile to my teacher's face. "Without a single word of condescension, I would encourage Judy, and calmly yet firmly I would simulate a long, hard, two-handed muscle contraction on her left calf until she came to her senses and apologized to me."

I said this with such confidence that the only response from the class was the hands of the two men being rapidly pulled back down, realizing they must have had the wrong answer. As I stood there looking sincere, the shock on Ms. Anzaloto's face was only surpassed by that on Judy's.

After a long, pregnant pause, I smiled just enough to say, "It's only a joke, folks," and they finally got it.

After all the practice and fun of the class, one week before the group's last meeting, the big day arrived. Early in the morning, our expected baby indicated to his sleeping mom with remarkable clarity he was ready to be born. And I was there.

I was there when he first shared the top of his head with the world. I was there seconds later when he nearly dove out, a little, slippery, purplish, four-and-a-half-pounder, sliding into the doctor's waiting hands.

Caught upside down by his ankles and frantically waving his arms, I watched his eyes open wide in horrified disbelief as the doctor permanently severed his old life support system. Then the doctor smacked him on the bottom, introducing him to his first smell of air.

I was there as he "flew," with his legs tucked tightly beneath him, on the long arc through surgical white light and down into his mother's open arms.

I was there as he lay on her moist, hot skin and tasted his first "home cooked meal." I was there!

After what seemed a very short time together, a nurse took our baby over to a piece of medical equipment that looked like the machine Burger King uses to keep the french fries warm. As she inked his hands and pressed them onto his record sheets, I congratulated Judy on the great job she had done. She wearily tried to tell me similar kinds of things.

"Mr. Stromberg," said the nurse still attending to the baby, "you'd probably enjoy seeing something here."

She held up my new boy's feet, and I noticed that both of his middle toes were webbed together.

"Well, look at that," I said with genuine delight. "Judy, his toes are webbed right up to the nail. Do you know anybody on your side of the family who has webbed feet?"

"Not that I can think of," she said dreamily. And then, "Doctor, is this something we should be concerned about?"

"Nah!" said the doctor. "He'll be a great swimmer."

And so he is.

***

We named our baby Nathan Isaak (God's gift of laughter). As I write this story, he is the twelve-year-old who has asked if I would please not tell any more stories about him. I explained that it is difficult for me not to write about my own family.

"Well, then," he said, "could you please not use my real name, Dad? It's just embarrassing."

So to avoid embarrassing my son by using his real name, I will for this rest of this story refer to him as Debbie.

***

Two years after his birth, we awaited another baby. Often I would say to people, "Of course we don't know the sex of this child, but we do expect to see some 'weberial webation.'"

As our little son Lars Eric made his journey into our world of light and air, once again I was there. As he cuddled on top of his mom, I dried his little body from his head right down to his surprisingly normal baby toes. What a thrill to see such obvious evidence that God had made both boys beautifully and uniquely themselves.

My children have been for me a wonderful demonstration of Psalm 139 where the psalmist says, "God, when I was still inside my mother's womb, You were molding me and forming me perfectly as I am. God, I praise You for Your marvelous handiwork!" (paraphrased).

To the psalmist's words I add my own: God, I thank You for the privilege of having a small part in my children's birth. Lord, I will praise You forever that as these marvelous works of Your hands entered our world, I was there.

CHAPTER FOURTEEN

HE WAS THERE

B oth my mom and dad were born and raised in the little town of Canoe Place. They became sweethearts at the Arnold Avenue School when it was still the junior-senior high. Every five years during my boyhood, they'd get all dressed up and go down to the fire hall or the lodge for their class reunion.

I always had the impression these were pretty big events, and the earlier ones probably were. But as the years went by, fewer and fewer people who had moved away were able to return. Some had good excuses (like death), while others probably just lost interest.

At their fortieth, only five other couples from their class of '44 came—and one guy from the class of '43 who got mixed up. At least that's what he said, though my mom thought he just went every year. Nobody cared. They let him stay.

In the early years, they probably talked about old times: last-second touchdowns, split trousers at the prom, cleaning up after the flood of '42. But every five years those memories became less important, and the talk turned toward family.

Where once dancing couples filled the fire hall, now thirteen people sat around two tables in the Canoe Place Inn, listening to a scratchy Glenn Miller recording and talking about the things most important to them.

"How's your mom doing since your dad passed away?" "I hear your daughter had twins. Oh, I'll bet Grandma's having fun." "Gilbert, what's your boy Gibby doing these days?"

When the conversation turned toward children, my folks began to wish they'd decided on a response before they came. It's not that I was an embarrassment to them; it's just that they didn't quite know how to answer the question "What's your boy doing?"

It was easy for the others. "Oh, Gibby's still doing brain surgery. Oh, yeah, he just loves it, can't get enough. Hard to believe seein' how he flunked biology twice and couldn't dissect a frog without passin' out. That's how he crippled up his hand so bad, ya know, faintin' head first right through that aquarium. Good thing, too, 'cause I could never have afforded to send him to medical school on my salary. His right hand still don't hardly move, but he says it don't bother him much."

Other children were teachers, lawyers, mothers and architects— all professions that were easily understood.

"Now tell me again, Lucielle, 'cause I can't remember," Gib, Sr., said to my mom, "what is it that your boy Bobby does?"

With a little laugh and a glance toward my dad, my mom passed the buck. "Well, you know, Gib, I'm not really sure. How would you answer that question, Bob?"

Ironically, this was fun for my dad—my dad the educator, my dad a past teacher and principal at the high school, my dad the Ed.D.

The truth is I *am* kind of a clown, and I always have been. The truth is I'll probably always earn a small portion of what my old classmate "One-Handed Gibby" makes repairing brains. And the truth is that what would seem a waste of skin to some parents is a delight to my mom and dad.

You see, they believe the psalmist when he sings: "God, when I was still inside my mother's womb, You were molding me and forming me perfectly as I am. God, I praise You for Your marvelous handiwork!" (paraphrased).

I love that passage mainly because the psalmist is the only guy I've ever known (more than four years of age) who truly recognizes himself for the marvelous creature he is. He even has the audacity to sing about it. Most of us are unable to do that. In fact, most of us spend a good portion of our lives wishing God had used His great and marvelous creative skill to craft us more wonderfully like someone else. I certainly stand guilty.

From the time I entered school, I began to feel uncomfortable with the body God had created especially for me. But I bought the thought that God wasn't finished with me yet, and perhaps He would even appreciate my helping out a little bit with the job. This kind of insight might have led me to deep theological study and personal introspection, but unfortunately instead it led me to the back of a Dell Comic book.

There, as a young teenager, I gazed in awe-inspired silence at the first "before" and "after" photos I'd ever seen. I could hardly believe my eyes.

The first photo showed a pale, eighty-seven-pound, shirtless guy in a baggy bathing suit cinched tight at the waistband, which rode high on his concave chest. Under the picture was printed the word *Before*.

To the right of this picture was another one of the same guy, but this time he must have weighed 210 pounds! He had oiled the deep

tan skin that enshrined his rippling muscles, which rose and fell like
the Allegheny Mountains. On each arm (literally on each arm!) sat
two lovely, bikini-clad beauties who looked as if they sat there often.
Under this picture was the word *After*.

I was inspired. To think that such a change could take place (and
in only twenty to thirty minutes) by drinking "Muscle Up, the Meaty
Drink of Champions"! I could hardly believe my eyes. These guys
didn't even look like the same person!

I took my small savings, ordered a case and learned an important
lesson about advertising. Apparently the ad didn't mean I would look
like the "after" photo in twenty to thirty minutes. The ad meant it
would take twenty to thirty minutes to drink a full glass. Then I
would spend twenty to thirty minutes alone in the bathroom, during
which time no beauties would volunteer to sit on my arms. So I
remained unhappy with this "temple" God had designed and built
without first consulting me.

I thought I'd found a solution during my first term in college. I
enrolled in a weight training class three days a week, two full hours a
day. The course cost $350, but it was worth it to me. After all, I was
not just getting a college credit, I was getting a new body, and with it
a whole new way of life.

But it didn't work, at least not the way I thought it would. Ten
weeks later, on the last day of class, I walked disgustedly into Coach
Phil Ed's office (we called him Fizz). I weighed four pounds less than
when I began and still possessed little motivation to oil my skin.

"Coach Ed," I said, trying hard not to look at the floor, "I want
my $350 back."

"I'd love to do that, Bob," said the coach, "but that would be an
infraction of the rules."

"Yeah, well, it didn't work," I said more boldly. "You told me if I faced
the pain, I'd find the power. And I believed you, but it didn't work!"

"Whoa, Bob. Time out!" he said, making a T with his hands. Placing his reading glasses on his nose and spreading my workout chart before us on his desk, he said sternly, "I'm afraid you're out of bounds here, Bob. You've stepped over the baseline, fella. You're offsides. Net ball!

"We can clearly see your progress," he said, pointing at the chart. "For example, right here where it says Day One, your maximum number of curls was three at two pounds. But today you did twenty-five at fifteen. In squats you were at . . . ."

Down the chart he went—curls, squats, bench press—and in every category I had made considerable progress.

"Is this what you meant?" I moaned. "Did you mean that if I went through these last ten grueling weeks, I would just get stronger?"

"You got that one right on the putting green, young man," he said. "What did you think I meant?"

"I thought I might *look* different," I protested. "I thought it might even change my body a bit."

"Whoa, Bob, you dropped the ball on that one. You ran the wrong pattern, tackled the wrong guy. Technical foul!" he shouted, making another big T. "You took the wrong course, Bob. You want a new body, that'll cost you another $350."

But my classes were already scheduled for the new term. I couldn't afford to pay the penalty fee to have them changed, and besides, I'd have to take the course from Coach Ed, who I always felt was playing the game of life about three yards short of a first down.

My feelings about my body were not something I talked openly about to people. It seemed better to keep my thoughts to myself.

I certainly didn't share them with my fiancé. She, after all, had agreed to marry and spend the rest of her life with me. I figured if she truly had not noticed I was a wimp, there was no reason *I* should put the thought in her head.

I suppose it was foolish for me to think I could have hidden my feelings for long. I will always remember the moment of truth, because it changed my life forever.

Judy and I were doing some shopping. I was looking for a new summer shirt, and not just any summer shirt, either. I wasn't too particular about color, but when it came to shape and size, I had some expectations. I had found that I felt pretty good about myself if I wore slightly large, boxy-cut shirts.

My theory was, if one wore a shirt larger than one's body, the shirt would not delineate that which it contained. Thus it was possible that a 400-pound person wearing a 500-pound-size shirt might not be recognized as fat but be seen as simply poorly fitted.

I was looking through a rack of rather large, Hawaiian-style shirts when I felt a tap on my shoulder.

"Hey, Bob," Judy said, holding a shirt for my consideration, "why don't you try this one on?"

On the hanger was a rubbery looking thing made out of spandex. The body of the shirt looked to be about five inches across the chest, and the arms were the dimensions of oversized drinking straws.

I tried to protest, but it was no use. Minutes later I stood, desperately alone, before the full-length dressing-room mirror.

Judy asking cheerily from behind the louvered door, "Hey, you in there, how's it look?"

"Not so great," I said, knowing what was coming next.

"Well, let's see."

Feeling nude, I opened the door.

To my surprise, her eyes lit up. "Oh, that's nice!" she said. And then wiggling her finger, "Turn around."

My life flashed before my eyes in an instant like one big "before" photo.

"Oh, I like it a lot!" she said. "Why don't we buy it?"

I couldn't believe what she was saying. How could she possibly like it?

"No, I don't think so, Judy."

"Why not? It really looks great on you."

"Oh, you know. I just really don't like the feel of it."

"But it looks so nice, and it's on sale, and you'd get used to it after a while."

"No, Judy, I don't think so," I insisted a little louder.

"Well, could you please just tell me why?"

Then I heard myself saying the words. "Okay, the truth is shirts like this have always made me feel kind of . . . skinny." Embarrassment heated my face.

"Skinny?" she said with a laugh. "Are you serious? Skinny? Bob, you're not skinny."

"Ah, come on, Jude; I know what I look like," I said, pointing toward the changing-room mirror.

Then she spoke words for which I had no argument, incredible words. Still, I had to believe they were true.

"Bob," she said, looking right into my eyes, "I love the way you're built."

I bought the shirt and walked out of the store reborn. The truth had set me free. The woman who loved me and whom I loved more than I could begin to express *loved my body*. For the first time in my life, I didn't care what anybody else thought. For the first time in my life, I didn't even care what *I* thought.

Some twenty years later, still shaped very nearly the way I was in college, I remain utterly transformed by her words, and I sing with the psalmist. After all, before I was born my Creator was there. He was there molding me inside my mother's womb. He was there delighting in my kicks and barrel rolls. He was there appointing the time of my birth, and at that moment He knew my name.

As my mother slept and my father stood behind glass gazing at a tiny baby (no doubt wondering who this child would be), my Creator was there, too. He was delighting in the genes and chromosomes, X's and Y's, all borrowed from my grandparents, perfectly knit together in my mom and dad and wonderfully crafted into the tiny bundle that was me, one day to be the miracle of my own children.

Oh, Wondrous Transforming Love, how marvelous You are!

CHAPTER FIFTEEN

THE BIG RETREAT UP THE BANGU

I s not so very big far," Tchimbalanga said in broken English, pointing through the jungle toward the sound of distant falling water. "I show. I show."

We climbed up the steep ravine farther into the dark green humidity. Tchimbalanga was truly the blackest person I'd ever seen, making me quite certain he was not from this part of the country.

Everyone else in the tiny village of Kempesi was short and stocky, with deep brown skin. But this man was easily 6′8″ and black as a biker's leather jacket. His feet might have been a size fourteen, but I could hardly imagine fitting them into any shoe. From his heel the foot spread out like a flipper, flat and wide from years of treading jungle trails.

"Wait!" I panted, my hands on my knees. "One minute, please!"

I'd been in Zaire exactly six weeks. I'd spent three out of the last four weeks flat on my back with malaria. It's the kind of disease that back in

117

the States they'd have you quarantined in your own wing of the hospital, fed with IV's and monitored 'round the clock.

But in Zaire, if you have malaria, people say you're just "dragging a bit" or you're "a little under the weather."

Regardless, malaria is scary the first time. As the missionaries say, "The first week, you hurt so bad you're afraid you might die. But by the second week, you feel so much worse you're afraid you might not."

"Okay, Tchim," I said, shaking the dizziness from my head and waving him on. "We go now."

Due to my illness, my French and Lingala studies had progressed slowly since my arrival in Africa. But my broken English was getting better every day.

"Is big long way more, hah?" I asked.

"No, no, my foot," he said with a laugh.

"You mean, no, no, my friend. This is foot," I said, pointing at the pods connected to the ends of his legs.

"This is friend," I said, pointing at my own chest.

Tchimbalanga threw his head back and let out a reedy laugh. "Oh, hah hah hah! Come! Come!" he said, pointing up the ravine. "Not so very big far, my french."

It didn't matter. We understood each other perfectly.

Even with my dull headache threatening an all-out assault, I was exhilarated to be there. Three months earlier I had been a single man, worried about final exams and unemployment. Now I was married, graduated and working as youth director of the International Protestant Church of Kinshasa, Zaire.

In a week, my new wife, Judy, and I would be taking our youth group on a retreat. I was hoping this little village of Kempesi would be the ideal spot. The village Catholic School of Pedagogy had agreed to accommodate us. The guest cottages were extremely primitive by even the campiest of American standards, but my youth group did not consist of typical American kids. Some were foreign embassy children, but most were from missionary families and used to roughing it out in the bush.

I knew it would probably be toughest on Judy, who had not had a great experience so far. Since stepping off the plane, she had struggled with the heat and humidity, which by comparison made August in Chicago seem brisk and invigorating.

On top of this, she was having difficulty dealing with the reality that her marriage was not as romantic as she had dreamed it would be. This reality was aggravated by having to play nurse to a delirious husband who crawled on all fours to and from the bathroom and had to be fed through a drinking straw for the last three weeks. To make things worse, most of our new friends were missionaries who had long ago made the tough cultural adjustments and didn't seem to remember the fears we were facing.

In fact, I became pretty convinced that missionaries were probably the most forgetful people I'd ever known. The first week after our arrival on the continent, the deacons at the church organized seven consecutive suppers for us in missionary homes.

Each evening the stories would begin over salads and fresh garden vegetables and continue through the chicken muamba (a delicious combination of chicken, palm oil and peanut butter gravy over white rice). The dish was surprisingly tasty, though not recommended for seven consecutive evenings.

At some point during the meal, our host would say, "So, are you starting to learn your way around?"

"Well, no," I would reply. "Actually, we're still waiting for our drivers' licenses. Until they come, we're pretty much stuck at home."

"Well, praise God for that!" our hostess would say, serving the gritty, powdered-milk ice cream. Then with a little laugh she'd add, "Believe me, the longer you're stuck at home, the safer you are. Why, you know, most of the drivers out there are little kids! Arthur, tell them what happened to Mary."

Each evening the names would change, but the stories remained much the same. Mary was back-ended by a ten-year-old cab driver whose uncle was a government official and demanded a payoff or Mary's family would be kicked out of the country.

Another guy named Jim stopped his car with the front bumper two inches over the crosswalk and was thrown in jail. Of course the phones didn't work, so no one in the church knew where he was. It took three days to find him. In Zaire, prisoners are fed by their families, but Jim was single, so Jim didn't eat.

The name Verner Pauls remained consistent through all seven evenings. Poor Verner's car was slammed from the side and shoved into a crowd of people. Verner wasn't hurt, but apparently someone in the crowd was. When he attempted to help, his car was over-turned, set on fire, and he was beaten to within a breath of his life. He was flown back to Goshen, Indiana, and no one expected him to return very soon.

Usually following a fairly detailed description of Verner's bat-tered body, someone would sensitively notice Judy's tension. Trying to steer the conversation in a more pleasant direction, that person would say, "Seen any big snakes yet?"

This would lead us into green mamba stories.

"Oh, yeah, deadliest snake in the world," our host would warn. "Why, they can kill a horse in three minutes!"

I hadn't seen a horse since coming to Africa, but everybody seemed fascinated by that three-minute equestrian statistic.

"Lucky for me," I'd joke each evening, "I didn't bring old Trigger."

" 'Course, if it bit you," my host would continue, raising his eyebrows and not missing a beat, "you'd be lucky to last thirty seconds. And you know, Bob and Judy, the really bad thing 'bout them mambas? They're soooooo long, why they'll go right up on their tails in the elephant grass eight or nine feet, and they'll wave back and forth just lookin' for ya. Most snakes you have to practically step on 'em before they'll bite atcha." (This was where they always got really excited.) "But these mambas, they're the most territorial snake in the world. The Africans tell 'bout how they'll actually come after ya, racing through the trees from a hundred feet away.

"Say, Helen," he'd shout to his wife in the kitchen, "what was that Bowan girl's name who got bit last Christmas?"

Then we'd hear all about little Lori, who would have been dead if she hadn't been bit in the fatty part of her bum and if her dad hadn't had serum right in the fridge and if the house boy hadn't chopped the mamba's long green head off in mid-flight just before it bit her again.

Our hostess would smile and ask, "More dessert, anyone?"

By the end of the week, we were nervous wrecks. I could convince Judy that the chances of a mamba offensive were slim since we lived in a somewhat urban area, but she'd also heard about baby vipers that come right in under the door.

Oh sure, it takes thirty days instead of thirty seconds before you die. But all the missionaries concurred that if you didn't get the right kind of serum, your head would turn yellowish gray and swell to the size of a watermelon.

Add to these fears the continual menace of cockroaches in the corn flakes, harmless but alien-looking gekko lizards in the dresser drawers and foot-long fruit bats singing us to sleep each night. We were beginning to question God's leading to the dark continent.

But now, nearly six weeks into our adventure, we were both still alive, had yet to see a snake, were becoming fond of our little gekkos and were adjusting to the idea that roaches had been with mankind from the very beginning. Besides, all our efforts to eradicate them would probably prove futile. Furthermore, Judy had been hired as a teacher's aide at the American school, which kept her busy during the hottest hours of the day, and physically I was beginning to bounce back from my fever.

The big fall retreat had been my idea. "Let's get the kids away from the city," I said to my youth committee. "Let's take them on a big adventure, something they'll be talking about all year long."

Of course the first question was "Where?" My young missionary friend John came up with an answer.

"How about Kempesi?" he suggested excitedly. "It would be perfect. The Catholic school there would probably house and feed us for a couple of bucks a piece, and from what I've heard, if we could get the kids up the Bangu to the upper falls, I guarantee they'd never forget it!"

John had agreed to drive the three and a half hours with me to make arrangements. He would have loved to hike up to the falls on a practice run, but unfortunately he had an infected bug bite of some kind that had swelled his knee up hot and red.

"Well, we'll just get someone else to show you the way," he said. "I don't think it's too hard to find."

So leaving just a bit before dawn, we arrived at the Catholic school in time for breakfast, where a priest introduced us to Tchimbalanga, who was thrilled to sell us an afternoon of his life for the equivalent of a buck seventy-five.

Soon Tchim and I were driving several miles over a rutted road to the base of the Bangu. John's enthusiasm had been inadequate to prepare me for the sight. Several hundred yards before us rose a wall of green earth a mile high, nearly vertical, and stretching left to right as far as the eye could see. Here, in ages long past, some mighty force of ice, flood or passing thought of God had caused the entire continent to drop off, and someone had uttered the name Bangu.

From where we stood, our heads back, shielding our eyes, it looked like a mountain range rising at our feet. But as John had explained, at the top began a gentle plateau that rolled inland for many miles.

My first thought was, *How on earth will we get seventy kids (all possessing little appreciation for their own mortality) safely up the side of that thing without ropes, picks and pitons?* Sensing my concern, Tchimbalanga motioned with his hand and said, "Come see!"

The entire trip to the upper falls was about three miles; one mile through ten-foot-tall, razor-sharp elephant grass; one mile of steep vertical ascent; and one mile over gentle plateau to the falls.

The first part was an easy walk, as there was a pretty well-worn footpath through the high grass. Though my instinct told me to keep an eye out for the deadly, swaying mamba, I was reassured to notice my guide seemed unconcerned, and I had yet to spot a dead horse.

The second mile was a lot tougher, as we climbed through an adder-like path of dusty brown switchbacks, probably doubling the actual distance. But forty-five minutes later, stopping to rest at the top, we could see well beyond the squalid village of Kempesi. I was beginning to imagine my celebrating youth group, standing triumphantly at this very vista.

"Not so big far," Tchim encouraged, and on we went. This time we traveled without a path on a straight line over dry earth, past towering, sculptured termite mounds like strange, earthen castles, and slightly downhill toward the green jungle ravine.

Though the day was oddly overcast, my face burned hotter with each step, my heart beat a slow thud of dull pain, and I looked forward to lying in a cool spray of water. Just before we entered the shade of the ravine, Tchim tried to impress on me the importance of entering at this particular spot.

"Good, good," he said, pointing toward a gentle slope leading down into the trees toward the sound of rushing water. "No, not," he said with a scowl on his face and pointed to our right toward what I assumed was upstream.

"Okay," I replied, not particularly caring. The trip had been easy, and I could see a mile behind across open plateau to the very spot we had climbed to the top of the path. There was little chance of getting lost. This was going to be easier than I'd hoped.

For twenty minutes I followed my guide as we climbed high along the wall of the ravine. Though an enormous volume of water cascaded noisily over a series of small falls far beneath us, the sound was insufficient to drown out the din of darting birds and screaming monkeys swinging through the branches above. This was truly an African experience.

At the top, climbing out of the shade into the brightness, before us like a postcard from Maui was the most beautiful sight. We stood on a sun deck of perfectly smooth stone, containing a deep pool of clear, cool water. Across from us rose a wall of rock easily fifty feet straight up, and over the top, between two large stones and through a spray of rainbow, spilled a graceful fall of sparkling water.

"Ah-ha?" Tchim asked, his shining face beaming with pride as if this spot were his very own.

"Oh yes! Yes! Very nice!" I exclaimed, stripping off my shirt and sliding into the cool pool as he squatted on the edge, rinsing his face.

The walk down was, of course, much faster than the hike up. The drive back to Kinshasa was thankfully uneventful, and Tuesday evening my youth group enthusiastically signed their names and turned in their money for the big fall retreat.

I was fired up! I'd counseled at camps and youth resorts all over the United States, from the California Sierras to Minnesota's boundary waters to the Adirondacks of upstate New York. But nothing compared to the exotic isolation of the Bangu. Several of the missions had volunteered buses and drivers, so Friday after school we drove off accompanied by the ever predictable irritant of "ninety-nine bottles of beer on the wall."

Besides this, the only other disappointment was John's knee, which had grown much worse during the week. Once again it seemed he would not be making the climb. But when some of the boys in the back of the bus heard this whole trip had been John's idea, they would not hear of his staying behind.

"If we have to, we'll carry him up there!" they swore.

Sure enough, on Saturday morning after breakfast, devotions and a couple of large-group games, the boys found a stretcher in the infirmary, and soon John lounged somewhat precariously atop their shoulders. As we hiked the first mile, John alone could see over the tall elephant grass. Gaining some confidence in his young bearers, he led the way like a king on his litter.

However, on the second mile, climbing the switchbacks, he chose to lie down and hold on as the boys, beginning to feel the heat, clawed and stumbled their way up the steep trail beneath their heavy load.

It was at this point I realized my first mistake. Tchimbalanga and I had made the climb on a relatively mild, overcast day, and we had arrived at the falls by 11:00 A.M. It was now almost noon.

I suspected it was well over one hundred degrees, and we were only halfway up the path. The hot sun had begun to fry the joy out of the group. The songs ceased, and the moaning commenced.

As Judy stopped to offer water to several kids who seemed only slightly less exhausted than she, I sensed a touch of anger in her voice. "Gee, Bob," she complained quietly, "how much farther is it?"

"Just to the top there," I said, trying to be upbeat but feeling a little nauseated myself. I joked in Tchim's accent, "Once we're up there it's not so very big far!"

No response.

By the time we made it to the top, a clutch of girls was crying inconsolably. One boy lay rolling on his back, moaning, with both calf muscles cramped up somewhere near his kneecap. Several of the brave boys carrying the stretcher (who had earlier spoken with such strong resolve) now lay face down in the dirt from partial dehydration and total ego collapse.

"Be sure to drink a lot of water," I cheered, trying to smile and hold on to any thread of loyalty and respect that remained. "Hey, gang, I'm sorry we got started a little late this morning. This clearly is not the time of day to attempt a climb like this, but you made it! Come on, gang, give yourselves a big hand!"

No one did.

"Okay, hey, I understand where you're comin' from, but it's not far now. Soon you'll all be lying under the waterfall of your dreams."

One of the youngest boys cheered, which would have been somewhat encouraging to me had the whole group not responded in unison, "Shut up, you little creep!"

"Okay, gang! Let's git 'em up and move 'em out! Rollin', rollin', rollin', keep them doggies rollin'," I sang, but no one seemed to hear me as they rolled over on their hands and knees and then up one foot at a time. Finally they stumbled forward, no longer single file but spread out across twenty-five yards, arms hanging at their sides like zombies.

"Well," Judy said, trying to rally my spirits, "you said they'd never forget this, and no one is going to accuse you of not delivering on your promise."

Then she added, "That is, unless they're already unconscious."

From behind us, I heard a surprisingly cheerful voice. "Anybody got an extra leg?" John stood balanced on one foot, his swollen knee useless.

"If you leave me here," he joked, laughing aloud at his predicament, "the vultures will have me picked clean by the time you get back."

"Okay, so we go with plan B," I said, draping his arm over my shoulder. The three of us adults hobbled after what had once been a fairly normal group of kids.

"Don't go into the trees until I get there," I shouted ahead.

Ten minutes later, I realized my second mistake. It had seemed unimportant when Tchim showed me where to enter the trees, but now I could see why he had pointed and said, "Good, good" and "No; not." Everywhere I looked, the undergrowth was so heavy we couldn't get into the ravine. Where was that spot? It had been so easy.

Looking back, I noticed I couldn't see where the path ended at the top of the climb, so somehow we'd gotten off course. I reasoned that we must have arrived at a spot a little too far upstream, which would mean that if we followed the edge of the forest down to the left, we should find the entrance.

But within fifty feet I encountered a long, impenetrable gully of tangled vine that left me with two options. Either we went back or we continued upstream, hoping to find another point of entry.

One look toward my youth group encouraged me to go on. They were spread out, squatting beneath bushes, stringy haired, with filthy faces that looked very much as if they belonged there.

"If we don't find that pool," John said with a giggle, starting to get a little giddy, "these beasts are going to start fashioning tools of destruction."

"Okay, buckaroos," I shouted jubilantly, which required every bit of thespian skill I possessed, "we're almost there. Follow me!"

For reasons I still don't understand, they did.

The entrance I found required us to crawl on our bellies for thirty feet through a tunnel of thick, green vine. Thankfully, the heat and fatigue had apparently drained away the primal jungle fears, for everyone submitted to my encouraging, "Come on, you can make it! Come on."

That is, until the last girl was halfway through.

Then one of the boys said, "Hey, did you hear what happened to little Lori Bowan last Christmas?"

The screaming scared a thousand birds from the jungle canopy, and I had to crawl back in the tunnel and literally drag the girl through by her feet.

For twenty minutes we walked through thick, relatively flat jungle in search of the ravine and its stream, which, I reasoned, would lead down to the wall of rock and spill over into our postcard pool. The shade had begun to restore some of the life to a few of the kids, which was a surprising disappointment to me. (I was starting to like them the way they were.) I could hear parts of conversation far back in the line.

"If she hadn't been bit in the bum, it would have been 'Good night, Lori,' " said a boy's voice.

Not caring to deal with any more panic, I shouted angrily, "Hey, Francis! Knock off the mamba stories! I'm not going to tell you again. You got it?"

"Okay! Okay!" he shot back. "I heard you, all right?"

All was quiet for thirty seconds, and then I heard him obeying the letter of my law. "Do you realize a spitting cobra can hit you right in the face from twelve to thirteen feet away? And if you don't rinse your eyes in milk within a couple of minutes, you can kiss your eyeballs good-bye, baby."

Another thousand birds fled their roosts.

Finally we found a small, murky, brown creek barely flowing off to our left.

"Bob," Judy said sarcastically, close to tears, "it's beautiful, just like Maui. Let's swim."

"If we follow this, it has to run into our waterfall," I said. "But, hey, let's take a vote. It's still only 1:45. Do you want to go back or continue? How many say we should go back?"

No on raised a hand.

"Good!" I said, feeling a little support. "Now, how many say we should continue?"

No one raised a hand.

"Good! On we go."

Forty-five minutes later, I silently admitted to myself we were desperately lost. At this point my third mistake became painfully evident. Why had I not enrolled in a college that offered a course in jungle survival for large groups of adolescents?

In Zaire it's pitch black by six o'clock. Through occasional holes in the canopy high above, I'd noticed the sun was no longer directly overhead. Scraping the mud from the face of my watch, I could see we only had another three hours before nightfall. Turning back was no longer an option. Even if we could retrace our steps upstream, the chances were slim we could find our exit tunnel of vine in the ever darkening jungle and reach the village before dark.

Through the whimpering, far behind me, I could hear only Francis continuing, "Of course, big constrictors are a whole different story . . ."

It no longer mattered. No one had enough energy to listen, let alone scream.

The only encouraging development was John's knee. He was feeling much better, walking on his own and, in typically good humor, joking that soon he'd be able to carry me. Then he whispered the suggestion we travel no more than another half hour before we break the news to the group about our change in sleeping accommodations.

Twenty minutes later I felt the powerful adrenaline rush of hope as the terrain began to change. Still barely moving, the creek was now just eight feet across and only six inches deep. It was still too murky to show its slippery, muddy bottom. The diminishing creek banks now disappeared and became nearly vertical walls of impenetrably dense jungle, rising a hundred feet above our heads. But only fifty feet downstream, at the end of this gauntlet, I could see the sun shining brightly on a pool of water that disappeared at the far end between two large rocks. "Dear God," I prayed, "please let this be the pool at the top of our waterfall."

"Oh, Bob," Judy said, "is that it?"

"Hey, you guys," one of the boys yelled back to the others, "we think we found it."

One last choice remained before me. Do we take the easy way and walk right down the middle of the creek, or do we try to burrow along the steep wall of thick, undoubtedly densely populated undergrowth?

It wasn't necessary to vote; I knew what the response would be. Down the middle we went.

Only fifty feet more, I thought, *only forty-five feet . . . only forty . . .*

From behind me I heard John's hushed voice, no longer cheery but oddly nervous. "Whoa, Bob, I don't like what's happening here."

"What's the problem?" I asked. "It's only about thirty-five . . ."

Then I felt another rush of adrenaline, but this one was a swelling fear, for the water was growing deeper with each step. "Thirty feet . . . twenty-five . . ." I said aloud, the creek rising to my waist. "Twenty-two . . . twenty . . ."

Once again the group was deadly quiet, as, single file, with cameras held high, the kids walked deeper into the murky brown stagnation.

I heard a familiar voice, "You know, water moccasins can swim right along the—"

Before Francis could finish, the two girls behind him had his head underwater, and the look in their eyes said, "He's not comin' back up."

"Let him live!" I shouted. "The dysentery he gets from the creek will be a more painful death than drowning. Fifteen . . ." up to my armpits. "Ten . . ." over my shoulders. "Five . . ." stretching my neck.

And then . . . Wham! The pain hit my ankle like an electric shock. My feet slipped on the muddy bottom, and without a breath or even a sound, I was under the water.

Whatever the creature was, its mouth was large enough to sink its sharp teeth into both sides of my ankle and pull me toward the pool. For several terrifying seconds, while I fought to regain some footing, it tugged hard on my leg. Then just as suddenly as it struck, it was gone.

Behind me, most of the group was unaware I'd even been missing. I broke the surface screaming. My eyes wide with terror, I thrashed past the line of stunned teenagers and shouted, "Get out! Get out! Get out!"

And they did. Seconds later, as I dove onto the creek bank, back at the beginning of the gauntlet, I turned to see seventy kids looking down through the jungle from a hundred feet above me, high atop the steep walls.

Thankfully Judy and John had both stayed behind and were examining the deep puncture wounds on each side of my ankle. All the missionary stories were coming back to me now like recurring nightmares. *How long would it be*, I wondered, *before my tongue went numb and my head turned color? Do you suppose I just imagined that dead horse under the water?*

"Well, you're lucky," John said with a laugh. "It wasn't a snake. Too many teeth. We're probably talking a baby croc." Before I could respond, Judy was halfway up the bank.

From above, the kids were pointing and shouting down to us excitedly, "Hey, you guys! We were going the wrong way! That wasn't our falls down there. It's right up here."

Moments later, limping, with my arm now slung over John's shoulder, we reached the top. The whole group was lying in the crystal clear upper falls.

The ordeal was over. We were all alive, and the kids, now refreshed and laughing, would sleep safely back in the village. I'd made some mistakes, but fortunately our adventure would end happily.

Unfortunately, I'm not too keen when it comes to learning from my mistakes. Too often in the years to follow, preoccupied by the world around me, I would not listen carefully to the Guide who knows the way to Paradise. Too often, denying that I was lost, with my options narrowed to a few, I'd take the easiest way straight down the middle, up to my neck in peril, with my eyes set on a goal that ultimately would not satisfy.

Fortunately, God has always loved me enough to turn me around.

The only permanent effects of my ankle bite would be Judy's life-long aversion to youth retreats. Our friendship with John would endure many years, and not one of the kids would ever think of the big weekend without a smile crossing his or her lips.

Even now, I can remember us in our jungle scene right out of Walt Disney, with my youth group frolicking in sparkling waters. Through the splashing and shrieks of delight, we hear a voice sounding clearly over the rest, "You know, you never find a baby croc alone."

A thousand birds fly out of the trees.

CHAPTER SIXTEEN

WHAT'S A PARENT TO DO

The first few months with our babies were peaceful. They slept cozily in their cribs, cooed in their car seats and bounced in their Johnny Jump Ups. We always knew where they were; if we didn't move them, they didn't go anywhere.

However, our anxiety increased proportionately to their mobility. What seemed like harmless objects to us became sources of pain and injury to our little scootchers. They explored their new world with a thirst for knowledge evidenced only in those who have yet to receive a report card.

The mere sight of an uncarpeted stairway made me shudder. All our empty electrical outlets were covered with plastic safety plugs. All our lower cupboards were latched from within, and anything that might become lodged in our babies' throats (say, anything smaller than a half gallon carton of milk), was moved out of reach.

133

These precautions did not stop our boys' relentless attempts to kill themselves. I remember our youngest son, Lars, repeatedly crawling under the coffee table at high speeds, only to discover the top of his head was higher than the top of the table. Ten or fifteen times an hour he reconfirmed this unchanging truth.

Day after day, week after week, he painfully tried to deny his own dimensions, which in reality were changing as the bump on his head grew ever larger. Yet stubbornly he would not fine-tune his movements to harmonize with the world around him. I called it the Chinese Coffee Table Torture.

I remember both boys' fascination with our black, cast-iron wood stove, which when fully fired on cold winter nights, glowed orange on the bottom. We barricaded the area with everything that would not burn, but this did not discourage our children. They had plenty of time and enjoyed the challenge.

"What better way to spend a day," they seemed to reason, "than to remove the obstacle piece by piece so we can melt our skin off?"

One proud parent, whose children were teenagers and still alive, had a solution.

"Listen, Bob," he said, "you want to keep your kids away from that stove? Well, then, let them touch it one time. They'll *never* touch it again."

I could hardly argue with that, seeing how, if I let them touch it one time, their hands would be gone.

Those were just a few of the dangers—and those were all indoors. Outdoors things got worse.

Our eldest son, Nathan, displayed little interest in walking through the first fourteen months of his life. (Fine with us.) Toward the end of that time, he could walk; he just didn't care for heights and was content to stay a little lower to the ground.

I noticed, though, each time I unlocked the front screen door, his eyes studied and his hands mimicked my every move. When he finally did decide walking was a viable form of transportation, he did not need to be taught how to unlock the door. Or how to stumble fifty feet down the driveway and into the road.

I'm talking about the road that looked like a New England meadow lane but was actually a state highway . . . the road that was posted at fifteen miles per hour but tolerated trucks pushing sixty. I had no difficulty catching him before he reached the road as long as I knew he was on his way, but what if I wasn't looking even once?

An older neighbor couple, the Silvers (whose children were grown and perfect), sat on our sofa and offered a suggestion. "Oh, Bob and Judy," gushed Estelle like the soap-product salesperson she was, "what you want to try is the diversion method."

"How does it work?" I asked.

"Oh, it's easy," said Sterling, hunting through his wallet for their latest family photo. "We sure can't complain about our kids. Can we, dear? Here's a picture of Sterling, Jr., hunting with our grandson Mercury and the dog Stainless. We diverted Sterling, and he did the same for little Quick—that's what we call him. I'll tell you, we just can't say enough about diversion."

"How does it actually work?" I asked.

"Well," answered Estelle in a soft voice, leaning forward as though she were about to tell me the secret to financial security, "when your child approaches the road, you simply divert him away. That's why they call it the diversion method."

"That's it?" I asked incredulously.

"That's it!" they said together. "It sure worked for us."

"No, no, you don't understand," I explained. "I know this child. I'll divert and he'll revert . . . or invert. Whichever one it is, you know what I mean. The kid'll vert on me."

"Yes, yes, of course he will," Sterling counseled, putting his arm around my shoulder. "But therein lies the beauty of this method. For you, Bob, are the adult. Soon your son will tire of your persistent, patient, non-aggressive diversions, and he will simply cease his destructive behavior."

Well, we tried it and proved to ourselves that the Silvers didn't know anyone in our family very well. For Nathan, it became a great game. He loved running away from Dad and toward the road, so Dad would chase him and turn him around, so he could giggle and run away from Dad again, so Dad would say "No, no!" and turn him around, so he could run away again and Dad would chase him and catch him and then he could get carried horizontally, high up under Dad's armpit, all the way to the porch where he could giggle and run away from Dad again . . . hour after hour after hour.

After supper, as I sat on the couch watching the evening news, he'd come up to me, looking very much like a dog with a stick in his mouth, and ask if we could go outside and "turn around." I hated the diversion method. With Nathan, diversion was a full-time job.

But then again, spanking would have been, too. It just didn't seem to bother him. I remember spankings as a child, and they hurt both my bottom and my pride. But to Nathan they just seemed confusing.

I'd spank the boy, and dry-eyed he'd look at me as if to say, "Father, I'm deeply concerned about the stress you've been under lately."

Pretty perceptive kid! I *was* starting to come apart. Every couple of months, while waiting in the grocery-store checkout line with a cart full of baby food and plastic diapers, a recurring tabloid headline caught my eye: "Mother Locks Children in Attic for Forty Years."

I actually found myself thinking, *Well, the kids might not have enjoyed it, but at least they didn't have to fall down the cellar stairs, get their tongues caught in an outlet, swallow a softball or get hit by a car.*

Of course, to consider this option would be ludicrous and even diabolical. To take away all freedom may save the body, but it destroys the soul, not something we as loving parents were anxious to do.

Fortunately, our problem with the road was solved. Unfortunately, it was solved by accident.

We had a cat (the key word here being "had"). The cat's name was Lucky.

One beautiful, early-autumn morning, with frost sparkling on the grass and maple leaves hang-gliding through a deep blue, cloudless sky, Nathan (then two and a half) came to me dragging his baby brother by the foot.

"Can me and Larsy go feed Hi Ho?"

"How do you ask?" I responded, playfully raising an eyebrow.

"Pleeeeeeez?" he sang, releasing his brother, who had not yet awakened for the day.

"Okay," I said, "ask Mommy for some carrots, and after breakfast we'll all go feed Hi Ho."

Hi Ho was the Silvers' horse.

Half an hour later, with Nathan pretending to push Lars in the stroller, the four of us walked down the driveway. Five feet from the end, Judy and I simultaneously spotted what I assumed was our cat lying in the road. It was hard to tell for sure, as Lucky was so much longer than usual.

Our own revulsion was overcome by concern that Nathan not see, but it was too late. Though he'd never experienced anything like this before, and though what lay stretching before us looked nothing like his kitty, Nathan's mind somehow reconstructed, from pieces of collar and paw, what had been a lifelong friend.

"Daddy, look!" he said, pointing.

"Oh, Nathan," I said with all the sadness I really felt, "poor Lucky went in the road and got hit by a car."

Holding tightly to my hand, Nathan led the way to the end of the driveway. Beginning at his feet, he slowly traced with his eyes a long path of cat down the road.

Without a word to me, he squatted and, punctuating with a pointed finger, shouted at Lucky, "BAAAAAAAAD! CAAAAAAAAAT!"

I never again had to tell him to stay out of the road.

I wish *I* learned as quickly. I, too, stand alongside a road. My heavenly Father patiently tries to divert me away, day after day after day. But it doesn't work.

I suppose He could take away my freedom so I couldn't choose to disobey Him, but He won't do that.

"Don't go in the road," He pleads. "If you do, you will die."

He doesn't say it to be cruel. He says it because He loves me, and He knows what the road will do.

But I don't listen. The road fascinates me, and even witnessing the death in the road of God's own child is insufficient to change my behavior.

What's a parent to do?

THE YEARBOOK

My yearbook hasn't been opened five times in the last twenty years, but you'd never know by looking at it. The back cover is gone; half the vinyl is torn from the front, exposing the thin cardboard beneath; and the binding is completely shot. To turn a page is to remove it.

In my family I was taught a respect for books, especially those of the hardbound variety. You always held them carefully. You gently broke in the binding. You never, ever dog-eared a page.

Unfortunately my puppy didn't share my respect, though he did possess a voracious appetite for good literature, literally devouring any book he could reach. He didn't go much for quick reads, either, preferring bigger, meatier books he could spend a whole day alone with and really sink his teeth into. So the pages have suffered some "water" damage, and in the faculty section, several teachers (though not the ones I would have chosen) have had their heads torn off.

I remember when I first held this book in my hands on a warm afternoon in the spring of '68. It was the annual yearbook assembly program, and cardboard boxes, each containing twenty-five books, were scattered around the football field. Beside each box stood a homeroom teacher and behind each teacher a line of excited students.

I loved this day and the anticipation of holding an entire school year in my hand. I loved seeing myself as I really had been. I loved the fun of hunting through each shot of the bleachers at the big game or the crowded hallways between classes, finding myself and exclaiming, "I think that could be me right there!" or "Oh, look, that's the back of my leg!"

I'd stood in lines waiting to get a book many times through my school years, but this was different. This was *my* book, *my* memories, *my* life.

Approaching the front of the line, two or three persons away from the cardboard box, I caught a whiff of the yearbooks' smell, like a new vinyl dashboard. Then Miss Sweeney put the book in my hands, and I stood with a thousand other students, leafing through in minutes what had seemed like my long sophomore year. I would have savored a moment alone to explore, picture by picture, page by page, but that would have to wait, for this hour was set aside for signatures. So our lines closed into circles, clutches of friends. The air filled with girlish squeals of embarrassment, and boyish displays of bravado. The students amoebically moved, joining and dividing, while some, unnoticed, sat alone.

Then the bell rang, and we went back to class, where I so wanted to open my new book and read all the wonderful things my friends had written about me.

Now, so many years later, I hold this ragged annual and read these little notes from my schoolmates, expecting that some emotional response will rise within, some twinge of nostalgic pain. But it doesn't happen. I'm amazed how distanced I feel from that time and place, so entirely set apart.

Oh, I do remember some of the signatures clearly.

Bobby, Bobby, Bobby. What can I say? To the very most bestest boyfriend I ever had.

Love you always, Sheila.

I remember this one because Sheila was a stunning beauty, and her words had a profound effect on me. For weeks I studied each line, confused, pondering the true meaning of love and wondering if she might ever consider trying me again.

But, in truth, Sheila and I had never been closer than the day she signed my yearbook. I mean this quite literally. We had never been *closer*. We'd never dated. I didn't even know she knew my name. I'd only said hello to her two or three times in my life. To this day I wonder how desolate her other relationships must have been if I was "the very most bestest."

Dear Strom, Well I guess you'll always remember one particular incident behind the Hogan, which I don't thing I better write about here. (Ha Ha, Hee Hee) See ya' round!

Your buddy, Buzz.

I remember my buddy Buzz, but I have no idea what the "one particular incident behind the Hogan" was that he's sure I'll never forget. It disturbs me just a little to know I did something so memorable, the kind of thing young boys still talk about when they're old men, but I can't enjoy it.

Bob, to a very coachable young man. Have a great summer and work on that left hand.

Coach B.

I tried hard to convince myself that "coachable" was equivalent to outstanding or talented or even most improved. But you don't get awards for "most coachable" or "most adequate right-handed dribbler."

The signatures go on.

As I look through the class pictures, I'm particularly struck that some of these people I've not seen or even thought about in the past two decades. If I hadn't looked at their pictures now, I might never have thought of them again. Back then I could have given every person's name without hesitation. Now I hold my hand over the names and mentally try to fill in the blanks beneath the pictures. I score maybe a high D.

My low score, at least for the underclassmen, might be explained by the 120 poorly lit, fuzzy pictures squeezed onto one page. But that's no excuse for the seniors.

The seniors have only four pictures per page. All the guys wear suits and ties, though a few have defiantly whipped their greasy, long hair high on their heads or combed it straight down into their eyes. All the girls wear V-necked, satin gowns that leave the very tops of their white shoulders bare. (I could never understand how each girl could have worn the exact same dress. I mean, what are the chances of that happening?)

Under each photo is the person's full name, an italicized nickname and that person's school career activities and honors (3 yr. football, 2 yr. basketball, 1 yr. debate, Nat. Merit Scholar), followed by a statement of each student's choosing, summarizing his or her philosophy of life. Most of these are quotes from Siddhartha, Nietzsche, or The Byrds. Though Steve Kinney chose "Woooo, Woooo, Woooo, Woooo" by Curly.

Twenty years later it all leaves me a little flat. This was supposed to be the book that would bring back a flood of memories. I flip through the pages now as if it's not even my own. Until I turn the page and see Jimmy.

I'm surprised he's good looking. I'd never noticed that before. It had never occurred to me he was a handsome boy, though by the time this picture was taken he was actually a *young man*. (This was at least his second senior picture, and I think he may have squeezed a couple of other school years into two as well.) He was what the system called a "special" student, though most just called him "slow," and many called him worse things.

But I can't see those labels in the picture. He really looks handsome and normal and even happy.

Beneath his photo is the full name James Albert Fink and beneath that the summary of his activities: 3 yr. projector club. That's all. Nothing more. No nickname. No philosophy. Beside his photo, carefully framing his face, is scrawled a message beginning "To Stromboli."

I remember painfully well when he wrote those words. I saw Jimmy that afternoon as I came out of the school's main entrance. He stood on the curb, facing the front of a long line of yellow buses, his right arm waving frantically, his left hand holding his new yearbook high above his head. Balancing precariously on tiptoes, craning his neck to see over the front of the bus and into the parking lot, he yelled, "Hey, Janet! Hey, Janet! Hey, Janet! Hey, Janet! Hey, Janet! Hey, Janet! Hey, Janet! Hey, Janet!"

Thirty feet away, pretty Janet Petrosky (who was in no way hearing impaired) climbed into a backseat and rode off with a gaggle of girls. Then he turned and spotted me.

"Hey, Stromboli!" (My friends called me Strom or maybe Stromie. Jimmy called me Stromboli.) "Hey, Stromboli," he screamed, fighting his way against the flow of students, "how do you like the new yearbook?"

"It's okay, Jimmy. I mean, it's great," I said quickly, realizing my last chance to escape was nearing, my window of opportunity growing shorter with each of Jimmy's awkwardly approaching steps. "Hey, listen, Jimmy, I have to go! Okay?"

But I missed it. He got his arm around me, and before I knew it, we were sitting together on the steps as 300 students walked past, filled the buses and then, with great amusement, pointed at me.

"Well, you know, Stromboli, I don't think you could really appreciate this book like me, you know? 'Cuz, like, you're not a senior and everything and like, in a way, I mean, it's like the seniors' yearbook. You know what I mean?"

"Right, Jimmy. Great," I said, embarrassed, almost succeeding in getting away from his long arm slung around my neck. "Listen, Jimmy, I have to go!"

"Stromboli," he sprayed, pulling me back down, "what's the problem?"

"My mom's picking me up," I pleaded. "I have to go to the dentist, Jimmy. Okay?"

"Hey, no problem," he said as if he understood perfectly. "But your mom's not here. Right?"

Jimmy stood and looked toward the end of the buses where several parents lined up in their cars, waiting for their kids. "So, hey, why don't you just relax a little bit till she comes?"

I was beginning to think I could not feel more embarrassed. Then Sheila walked by.

"Shee-Lah!" Jimmy shouted with an inflection that made her lovely name sound like a hog call. "Hey, Sheeee-Lahh, you want to sign my new yearbook?"

Not surprisingly, she didn't turn around.

"Listen, I have to go, Jimmy. My mom's gonna be—"

"Hey, let me show you somethin', Stromboli," he said with a giggle. "This is unbelievable, I mean *on-believe-a-bull*! Did you see the picture of Conners? Did you?" He licked his fingers, leafing frantically through the pages.

"No," I said, "I really haven't had a chance to —"

"We're talkin' *on-believe-a-bull*." He poked the picture. "Look it here!"

It was a picture of Mrs. Dunn's Senior Boys' Quartet. Nothing struck me as being particularly unbelievable. Mrs. Dunn stood behind the piano with one hand on the keys and the other directing her four boys, who sang a long-O vowel sound. I had not a clue why Jimmy sat beside me laughing, but then again I really didn't care.

"Yeah, great, Jimmy," I said impatiently. "Listen, I really have to go!"

"No, no, Stromboli, you don't get it, do you?" he said, his left arm pulling me closer, his right hand pointing carefully at the picture. "You see Conners? Do you see him right there?"

He giggled excitedly. "Look at his face real close."

"Yeah, okay, I see him, Jimmy," I said, trying to break loose, as eight long, yellow buses with forty-five snickering students each, drove past.

Trying hard to hold back his laughter, Jimmy practically had me in a headlock, his face about three inches from my own. "Well, the day that picture was taken, Stromboli, after lunch Conners came to class, you know? And he like was feeling kind of sick to his stomach, you know? And he could have made it out of the room, but for some reason, I don't know why he didn't, you know? And he just kept getting sicker and sicker and sicker until finally . . ." Now he could hold it in no more, pursing his lips in a spray of laughter, "Right in the middle of 'The Impossible Dream,' Conners like tosses his lunch all over the piano, all over his sheet music. Oh, Stromboli," he said, wiping tears from his eyes, "you should have seen it. It was so great!"

I couldn't believe this was happening to me. Where was my mom?

"Is that unbelievable or what?" he howled and then added, quite seriously, as if the detail might hold some special significance for me, "It was mostly corn."

I managed an unenthusiastic, "Yeah, Jimmy, unbelievable."

I thought the worst was probably over now. The parking lot was empty except for a few faculty cars and some straggling junior-highers waiting for the late bus. Surely my mom would be pulling in any minute and apologizing that, for the first time in my entire life, she had completely forgotten about my appointment.

"Hey, Stromboli," Jimmy said, "check out this picture of The Kid."

I knew all the nicknames—Hondo, J.B., Zippo, Night Train, Mudman—but I'd never heard of The Kid.

"Who?" I said.

"The ah . . . The Kid," he answered nervously.

"Jimmy," I asked, for the first time genuinely interested, "who's The Kid?"

"You know, The Kid." And then, almost ashamedly, with his eyes suddenly unable to look into my own, he stammered, "Sometimes I ah . . . well, you know, sometimes I call myself . . . The Kid."

Before him was his photograph and beneath it his full name. His voice had changed now, as he studied his own portrait. "How you like it, Stromboli?" he said proudly.

"It's ah . . . it's nice, Jimmy," I answered, embarrassed that he'd asked the question.

"Yeah, well, it would've been a lot better if I hadn't got that black dot right in the middle of my nose," he complained, pointing at his own face and crossing his eyes. Sure enough, it wasn't big, but there appeared to be a pencil mark right on the tip of his nose. "I talked to Craig Donley, the editor of the yearbook, you know? And he said it wasn't his fault 'cuz it like happened when they printed the book."

Jimmy sat there staring at me, waiting to hear me say the dot was an accident, waiting for my reassurance that this was not just one more in the long litany of my school's practical jokes on Jimmy the Finkster. I wasn't at all sure it hadn't been put there intentionally, but if it had, it sure wasn't my responsibility to tell him.

I tried a feeble, "Oh, yeah, Jimmy. Hey, it probably happens all the time."

To my relief, I saw our blue Chevy pulling into the parking lot. "There's my mom!" I said, grabbing my books. "I have to go." But he had my jacket by the arm, pulling my sleeve down over my hand. "Wait, Stromboli," he said with something of desperation in his voice.

Then, letting go of my arm, he held his yearbook out to me with both hands, and in barely more than a whisper he asked, "Do you want to sign it?"

The truth is I didn't. The truth is I was angry. For one thing, I was already late for the dentist, but even more, I didn't know what to write. I mean, what do you say to a guy like Jimmy? He's not the kind of person you want to encourage with kind words, because if you do he's on your doorstep the next morning wanting you to come out and play. He's like the abandoned, oversized puppy that follows you everywhere you go, trying to lick your face. And he doesn't mind jumping all over you, clawing your body and soiling your clothes to do it. If I signed his book, everybody in the school would hear how "close" we were, how we were "best of friends." Next thing I'd know, he'd be wanting a date with my sister!

But there he stood, holding out his book, searching my face, waiting for an answer. My mom beeped the horn, "Quick! Quick!"

"Okay, but hurry!" I snapped, rolling my eyes and grabbing his book. "My mom's waiting, all right?!"

"Hey, Stromboli?" he asked, this time so softly I could barely hear the words, "Ah . . . ah . . . you probably want me to sign yours too, huh?"

I really didn't care. "Hurry!" I shouted, shoving the book into his chest with no attempt to disguise my anger. But then, as I leafed through the pages hunting for my picture, without warning my anger kicked back at me like a dull chain saw cutting deeply, leaving me stunned, staring blankly and unable to move.

I couldn't believe it. The pages of his yearbook were perfectly clean. There were no signatures. Not even one.

I lifted my face to see him looking at me, and I knew he'd seen my shock.

"Stromboli, I have to tell you," he recovered, almost believably shaking his head in disgust. "Your book is really a mess. I can't stand it when people write all over their faces, you know? That's why I only asked a few special friends, like you, to sign it. 'Cuz, like, when you're a senior you don't like to ruin it, you know?"

"Yeah, I know what you mean," I said, confused by the emotion I had not expected. "I kind of wish now I hadn't made such a mess of mine." I knew it was a lie, but it was the best I could do.

Jimmy handed me my book, and as I returned his, I pointed toward my mom and said, "Jimmy, I have to go."

I thought I pulled it off. I was pretty sure Jimmy thought he fooled me with that talk about not wanting people to sign his book. I crawled in the car, and my mom drove me away.

Now, more than two decades later, long removed from the awkwardness of that spring day, I hold in my hand a page from my old yearbook. On it I see James Albert Fink's handsome portrait. Framing his face are the carefully printed, still surprisingly disturbing words that catch my heart off guard:

> *To Stromboli, You are a great guy! Don't ever change.*
> *Your friend, Jimmy, The Kid.*

Lifting a pen to the page, I write beneath his words:

> *Dear Jimmy, We aren't always who we appear to be.*
> *Stromboli.*

THE ZIPPIEST TESTIMONY EVER

I considered it my first *real* job. Oh, I'd brought in hay for a few summers and even did an after-school stint potting geraniums and mixing manure at Larsen's Greenhouse.

But these jobs seemed like small change now that I'd been hired as a dishwasher at Camp Mission Meadows. The pay wasn't the greatest ($18.50 a week), but I got all my meals and a bunk in a cabin with the other "rags," and we only worked five or six hours a day. Furthermore, I could spend my entire summer on a beautiful lake far from home with fun people who were my age. Not a bad deal for a fifteen-year-old kid.

During our first staff meeting, our camp director asked if one of the dishrags would be willing to share a word of testimony at our Friday evening camp fire. Several of us volunteered, and my buddy Mike was chosen. The rest of us didn't mind him going first. We all knew we'd get our chance.

I didn't have another thought about it until the camp fire that Friday night, when I realized I was in trouble. As Mike gave his testimony, I sat on a log staring at the ground, certain my blushing would be detected even through the fire's glow.

For the first time in my life I realized what a testimony was. It was embarrassingly evident to me I didn't have one.

Mike's story was the first of its kind I'd ever heard. Only a year earlier, he'd been three thousand miles from home, drunk and unconscious, face down in a gutter, wishing his life would end.

But, as Mike put it, "God had different plans."

People he'd never met pulled him out of the street and into their shelter, where he was nursed back to health, delivered from his addiction and introduced to "the real thing," life in Jesus Christ. From that moment on, Mike had become "like a brand new person."

"Praise God!" he said, holding up his hands. "Praise God!"

All was silent except for the unanimous sniffles and the snap of the fire.

Mike's was a story of bondage to freedom, death to life, darkness to light, hell to holiness. It was a story nothing like my own, and I knew I was in trouble. So this was what our director meant by testimony.

I knew how many "rags" there were, and I knew how many weeks of camp there were. I didn't even need a pencil and paper to know my moment at the camp fire would come.

Oh, what I would have given for a *real* testimony! What I would have paid to stand confidently by the smoky fire with tears in my eyes and say, "Let me tell you my story."

Frogs would fall silent. Noisy boats would turn and go the other way. Junior high campers' mouths would gape wide, and the kids would lean forward, not wanting to miss a single word.

"Shhhhh! Shhhhh!" they'd say. "I've heard this is great!"

Softly but firmly, I would begin. "It all started late last fall, when I was fourteen. Unbeknownst to my parents, for several years I'd been dating Dolores, a senior cheerleader from Indiana State University. I'm ashamed to admit it now, but I used to steal my father's car after he and Mom went to bed. I'd drive three and a half hours to the Pennsylvania-Ohio border, where she'd meet me, and we'd experiment with mind-altering drugs. Then I'd drive home just in time to hop into bed before my parents got up.

"I know this probably sounds great to you kids. I thought I was really living. I thought I had it all, until one night . . ." (I'd be crying now) "one night . . . , well, I guess you could say I lost my head.

"I was driving back home without a license, high on lighter fluid and going about 120 m.p.h. Without warning, a runaway F-15 fighter jet came beneath the tree line, sheering off the top of the car and my head.

"At the time I remember thinking, *Uh-oh, this could be it!* But now I know the doomed fighter jet was sent from God, because somehow I found my head on the floor and had the presence of mind to put it on the dashboard so I could see. I drove about forty miles (I'm not sure about the actual distance, because I wasn't feeling too well). I found a tiny, rural hospital where a medical team of specialized neck surgeons sewed my head back on.

"Ever since that time, I've been praising the Lord. Alleluia!"

Oh, to have a testimony like that. To have a testimony I could send to *Guideposts*. But I didn't have one. Though the others weren't all as good as Mike's, they were all better than mine, and I knew I was in trouble.

On the last Tuesday of the summer, our director asked, "So, who's left?"

Head down, I raised my hand. "Oh good, Bob, you get the last night of the summer. I was afraid we'd have to start over."

"Oh," I said too quickly, "that would be fine. I mean, if you wanted to . . . start over, I mean."

"Is there some problem?" he asked.

"No, no!" I said trying to gain some composure. "Whatever you want to do is . . . that would be fine. I mean, great . . . really!"

I knew I wasn't doing well.

"Bob, if there's some problem with you offering your testimony, we can sure talk about it."

"No, no, no, no, there's no problem," I said, and then added, "Would you like me to do Mike's? I mean, is it legal? I could probably pull it off."

Later in his office, nervous, embarrassed and picking at my fingers, I told him my story. It *was* nothing like Mike's.

I was only five or six years old. I'm not sure about my actual age, because I didn't know it was important to remember a date. I sat in the parsonage's musty basement at a tiny table with two other boys and my Sunday school teacher.

I remember she told us how much God loved us even though we disobeyed Him. She told us how God decided to come to earth as a baby named Jesus. She told us how Jesus grew to be a boy and then a man (just as we would be someday), but He never ever sinned as we had. She told us how He allowed Himself to be killed not for His own sins, because He had none, but for her sins and ours, too.

And, she told us, He didn't stay dead. But He came back to life to offer us a free gift of special, everlasting life. We only had to pray and accept it.

She asked us if we would like to do that, and I said yes. That was it — no drugs, no pain, no doubts.

I guess I passed the audition, because I told my testimony at the camp fire, and I'm glad I did. I think that last night of the summer was the best one. It helped me to understand my story is no less miraculous than Mike's, for the miracle in my life is not the gutter God pulled me *from*, it's the gutter God *kept* me from.

CHAPTER NINETEEN

FACING THE MUSIC

Nearly four thousand people packed the intersection and connecting streets, lining every stairway, windowsill and rooftop. Some had traveled for days.

Three mangy dogs, trotting by on their daily scavenge, glanced warily from side to side and then, almost as an afterthought, darted at a brood of squawking chickens, scattering them into the crowd. One bird, wide-eyed and caught up in a snarling jaw, screeched as its owner kicked the dog in the ribs, rolling it through the dirt, stirring up a cloud of dust.

"Hey! Hey, git! Git out! Git out!" voices shouted.

The mutt released his damaged prize and yipped away, with his tail between his legs and a pack of hollering boys, wielding long sticks, in hot pursuit of him.

People had just taken their places, sitting in the dirty street,

153

their knees pulled in close, when again they rose with angry curses, directed toward a man leading two oxen right through the middle of the intersection.

Farther back someone shouted at them, "Down in front!"

"Oh yeah? Well, why don't you just walk over here and make me?"

One young mother in a tearful panic searched the crowd for her little boy, crying, "Joshua! Joshua!" while down a side street another mother dragged her screaming Reuben by the ear.

Barking, squawking, screaming, bleating, cursing. Just another typical audience for the young teacher who raised His hand and watched as a deep silence fell on His crowd.

When all was quiet (even flocks and herds), in a soft, gentle voice that surprisingly carried clear to the back row, Jesus said, "Be on your guard against the yeast of the Pharisees, which is hypocrisy. There is nothing concealed that will not be disclosed, or hidden that will not be made known. What you have said in the dark will be heard in the daylight, and what you have whispered in the ear in the inner rooms will be proclaimed from the roofs" (Luke 12:1a-3, NIV).

Scripture does not confirm it, but I'll bet at least one of those who had walked two days and slept in a ditch to be there wanted to cry out over the crowd, "Say it ain't so, Lord! This isn't what I came to hear. I mean, who among us doesn't smell just a little bit yeasty? And now you're saying that someday we have to stand up in front so everybody can take a good whiff? No thanks! Come on now, Rabbi, give us a little gospel."

But Jesus said what He said, and I have little choice but to believe it's true. I try to envision that day when all my hypocrisy and lies and lust and idol atry and curses and murder and hatred and gossip are laid bare for the world to behold, but I can't do it. My senses just shut down.

At first it seems there's nothing in my experience that helps me to imagine this horrible event. Then, far back in my memory, I hear a whisper, "Remember the Christmas concert?"

The truth is, I'd rather not.

In my little town, the excitement surrounding the annual school Christmas concert was surpassed only by the excitement surrounding Christmas itself. All nine hundred of us in the elementary grades began to rehearse our music during the first week of school, which felt pretty odd.

"I'm dreaming of a white Christmas," we sang in September, as the mercury climbed toward ninety-five degrees. "Chestnuts roasting on an open fire," we fluted in October, as the sweet smell of burning leaves beckoned beyond the playground. "We wish you a merry Christmas," we rooted in November, like a cheer at the last home football game. And then, what do you know, it was December, and the pressure was on.

"You've got to sing, children!" Miss Nagle would shout, wiping the sweat from her brow. "I cannot do it for you. All your parents are coming to the concert, and if you just stand up there and mumble, it is you who shall feel foolish, not I."

This was a lie Miss Nagle told us each year for motivational purposes, and it worked pretty well. Most of us didn't want to feel foolish, so we sang a little louder.

Of course, we then discovered the truth was the exact opposite. When you are one of nine hundred mumblers, you don't feel foolish if you're mumbling; you feel foolish if you're singing. On the other hand, if you are the director of a nine-hundred-voice children's choir singing, "Cheznuz rozin' onnon obenire," now that's embarrassing!

"Look at me, children!" she would snap.

Whenever Miss Nagle said "Look at me," I would feel little giggle bubbles of delight growing somewhere deep within my chest. How could we help but look at her? If she was in the room, we were looking at her, for all else was hidden from view. She was enormous and, for me, a marvel to behold.

Each Tuesday and Thursday at 10:33, our second-grade teacher, Mrs. Bonner, would smile cheerily and say, "Students along the wall, it's time to move your desks now. Miss Nagle will be here soon."

Then my row would stand in unison and push our desks two feet toward the center of the room so Miss Nagle could fit past. This did not seem at all odd to me. I thought all music teachers were made like mine.

Soon, three hundred pounds of Miss Nagle would turn sideways and ease through the door. She was only 5'5", but she carried her weight with pride, wrapping it in elegant, stretchy knits. She wore her yellow hair high on her head with a shape and texture like spun cotton candy. A priceless jewel was set in each corner of her glasses, she had perfectly applied color on her ruby lips, and at the base of her many chins, rested a string of pearls that looked as if they connected her head to her body.

Most fascinating to me was the vast contrast in textures represented in one person. Each music class, when she bumped me going past, I could feel her meaty left hip, hard and tight as a trampoline. But when she stopped walking at the front of the room, other, softer parts of her body would keep moving all by themselves.

One day, as she stood still at the blackboard adjusting the five pieces of chalk in her music staff stick, I counted as the fatty bags behind her arms, big as milk bottles, swung back and forth eighteen times. It was always fun to look at her.

"Look at me, children!" she would snap. "Now sit up straight and sing it like this."

In my little town, the only exposure we'd had to operatic singing was Bugs Bunny, so we associated her classical sound with laughing, which is exactly what we did when we tried to sing a tune as she had. It was impossible for thirty second-graders with laughter bursting out their nostrils to sing well.

So all nine hundred of us felt a little nervous that December evening in 1959. We quietly sat in our classrooms, waiting to walk in long lines down the hallways and onto the auditorium stage, where we would mumble our songs and feel foolish in front of all our parents, just as Miss Nagle had promised.

"Sing out, children!" she whispered harshly with a severe smile as we walked through the backstage door, behind the curtain and onto the bright auditorium stage. "It's up to you! It's too late. I can't help you anymore."

The sixth graders had already stood on the top riser for nearly ten minutes as I took my place center stage, second row from the front. We waited for four classes of first graders and four more of kindergartners to fill the first two rows. When the last five-year-old found his place at the end of the front line, our parents burst into applause.

I felt sure Miss Nagle was beaming with pride. We had yet to sing a note, and already they were clapping.

Mr. Pelegrini, our principal, approached the microphone. "Merry Christmas!" he shouted and then jumped away as feedback screeched through the auditorium, eliciting screams of laughter from the choir.

"Let's try that again," he said softly and then, jokingly covering his ears, just in case, sneaked up to the microphone.

He whispered, "Merry Christmas."

Everyone laughed.

"I thank you all for coming this evening," he continued and then motioned toward the curtain. "Now would you welcome our choir director, Miss Nagle."

Everyone clapped as we stood at attention awaiting her entrance. But she did not come. We stared in silence at our parents, as our parents stared at us. A couple of kindergarten kids waved, and then one of them yelled, "Mommy, did you bring Grammy?"

Again everyone laughed, but still no Miss Nagle.

Then the backstage door flew open, and the whole choir turned to see our director behind the curtain, frantically tucking in her blouse and adjusting her skirt. Finally satisfied she looked her very best, she raised her chin, loudly mouthed the words "Sing out!" and, with a smile, walked into the bright lights. The applause carried her to center stage, where she turned toward the audience and bowed.

At this moment all nine hundred of us saw the problem clearly, though many of us were not at all sure what it was. Somehow, Miss Nagle had tucked the bottom of her skirt into the top of her girdle. Before us, indescribable (actually, undecipherable) to a second-grader, was an abstract sculpture of dimpled flesh, straps, nylon stockings and lots of white material like rubber bathing caps. I really couldn't tell for sure what I was looking at, but I sensed it ought not to be on stage.

The same boisterous little kindergarten girl managed to say quite loudly, "Miss Nagle, your—"

But before she could finish, Miss Nagle spun around with her finger pressed to her lips, raised her baton and lead us straight into "Deck the Halls." I don't think we sang it very well. Speaking for myself, I was so preoccupied with the commotion in the front rows I pretty much stuck with the "Fa-la-la-la-la's" right through the verses.

Through the last half of the song, a lady standing on tiptoes down below reached onto the stage and tapped the floor near Miss Nagle's feet. But Miss Nagle, more animated than I'd ever seen her, didn't seem to notice. As far as I could see out into the audience, women sat as if stunned, with hands over their mouths, and men hid their faces in their laps.

What seemed many moments later, finishing the song with one last "Fa-la-la-la-la, La-la-la-la," Miss Nagle turned and bowed again. This time to deep silence, broken only by the little girl shouting, "Miss Nagle, your bottom's showing!"

Most of Miss Nagle froze, though some parts before us continued to move. Another lady made her way quickly onto the stage and, with one little movement, released the skirt and helped it cover what had been exposed. It was only then, with a rush of blush, that I fully realized what I had been staring at. Miss Nagle turned back toward us and smiled as tears pooled in her eyes. "Sing out," she mouthed, this time quietly, and we did.

While tears rolled down her cheeks, we sang as we'd never sung before. Though each song was followed by thunderous applause, she did not turn around to acknowledge it.

At the end of the program, she placed her hands over her heart and smiled at us as if to say, "Very good, children. Thank you." Then she tried to lift her chin, but somehow she couldn't. With eyes lowered, she turned and left the stage.

On the way home, sitting in the back of the car, I heard my mom say sadly to my dad, "Oh, I feel so badly. The poor woman."

I don't remember hearing another word about it for probably ten years. Then it came up again around a big family meal where we laughed until we cried. But we stopped as quickly as we'd begun, remembering how terrible it must have been for Miss Nagle, how awful to nakedly expose so much of what she had most wished to remain hidden.

Maybe it's still difficult to laugh about it because somewhere deep inside, we all know we'll have to stand up someday like Miss Nagle and face the music. Maybe somewhere deep inside we know that, for us, it will be worse.

But this does not cause me to feel afraid. For when all that I've hidden is revealed, when all that I've said in darkness is heard in the daylight, and all that I've whispered is proclaimed from the rooftop, my Creator will ask, "Bob, is this all true?"

And I will answer, "Yes, Lord, every word."

He will ask, "Then are you condemned?"

But I won't have to answer, because I will hear a voice saying,

"No, Father, not condemned. These are the very sins for which I shed my blood."

And Jesus will wrap me in His arms, and we will walk off to share eternity.

AN ANSWER TO THE QUESTION

I am continually asked, "Are your stories really true?"

I usually respond as Tony Campolo once did to a similar question, "Well, if it didn't happen this way it should have."

Of course, I understand that if you're asking the question, that response is not very satisfying. The truth is that most of these stories are true precisely as told, though many contain slight embellishment and a couple contain a little more than that. For example, "The Bee Bagger" is almost pure fantasy, though even here there is much truth, including some information about the town, my musical interests, my grandparents and even my discovery that you can mechanically empty a hive. But the storyline is true only in my mind, where, if I'm not careful, I can easily begin to believe it really happened.

I hope this answers the question, because I'd prefer to be no more specific, though I will give a clue to those of you who would persist: The stories you think could not possibly have happened just the way I tell them ("Miracle at Stinky Bay," for example), did.